Easy-Care Guide t Houseplants

CREATIVE
HOMEOWNER®

Easy-Care Guide to
Houseplants

Jack Kramer
Principal Photographer: David Van Zanten

CREATIVE HOMEOWNER®, Upper Saddle River, New Jersey

Editorial Director: Timothy O. Bakke
Art Director: W. David Houser
Production Manager: Kimberly H. Vivas

Senior Editor: Neil Soderstrom
Editor: Nancy T. Engel
Associate Editors: Robin White Goode, Heidi Stonehill
Consulting Editor: Jacqueline Murphy (plant problems)
Contributing Editor: Anne Halpin (bulbs, herbs)
"Easy-Care" Inspiration: Kathie Robitz
Photo Researcher: Amla Sanghvi
Editorial Assistants: Craig Clark, Laura DeFerrari,
              Dan Houghtaling, Dan Lane,
              Sharon Ranftle

Cover and Interior Book Designer: Melisa DelSordo
Illustrators: Vincent Alessi (leaf and petal color wheel)
       Steve Buchanan (grow-light stand)
       Michael Gellatly (plant hanger installations)
       Roman Szolkowski (culinary herbs)
Front-Cover Photo Stylist: W. David Houser
Front-Cover Photographer: Alan Detrick, ALD photo inc.

Printed in the United States of America

Current Printing (last digit)
10 9 8 7 6 5 4

Easy-Care Guide to Houseplants
Library of Congress Catalog Card Number: 98-89442
ISBN: 1-58011-063-0

CREATIVE HOMEOWNER®
A Division of Federal Marketing Corp.
24 Park Way, Upper Saddle River, NJ 07458
Web site: www.creativehomeowner.com

Safety First

All projects and procedures in this book have been reviewed for safety; still it is not possible to overstate the importance of working carefully. What follows are reminders for plant care and project safety. Always use common sense.

- *Always* consider houseplants poisonous to eat. Some parts of plants are always poisonous to people and pets, while others may be poisonous, or at best cause indigestion, in people and pets. If there is a chance that children or pets will eat parts of houseplants, be sure to position the plants safely out of reach. The author and the publisher accept no responsibility for injury resulting from ingestion of any plant mentioned in this book.

- *Always* consider the possibility that houseplants may cause skin reactions in people with allergies. Some plants, such as those from the euphorbia genus (including poinsettias) give off a milky sap that can cause skin problems and eye injury. Also it's wise, especially for beginners, to exercise caution in handling unfamiliar plants. Gloves can provide protection, although glove exteriors will likely continue to be contaminated. Washing your hands after plant care helps prevent transmission of plant substances. The author and the publisher accept no responsibility for any injury resulting from the handling of plants mentioned in this book.

- *Always* ensure that the electrical setup is safe; be sure that no circuit is overloaded and that all power tools, lights, and electrical outlets are properly grounded and protected by a ground-fault circuit interrupter (GFCI). Do not use power tools in wet locations.

- *Always* read and heed tool manufacturer instructions.

- *Always* wear eye protection when using chemicals, sawing wood, drilling wood, and using power tools.

- *Always* consider nontoxic and least toxic methods of addressing plant pests and diseases before resorting to toxic methods. When selecting among toxic substances, consider short-lived toxins, which break down quickly into harmless substances. Follow package application and safety instructions carefully.

- *Never* employ fungicides, pesticides, or other chemicals unless you have determined with certainty that they were developed for the specific problem you hope to remedy.

- *Always* read labels on chemicals, solvents, and other products; provide ventilation; heed warnings.

- *Always* wear appropriate gloves in situations in which your hands could be injured by rough surfaces, sharp edges, thorns, or poisonous plants.

- *Always* wear a disposable face mask or a special filtering respirator when creating sawdust or working with powdery gardening substances.

CONTENTS

Introduction: About This Book 6

Part I: A World of Plants 8

1. FOLIAGE, FLOWERS & FAMILIES 10
   Conditions in Your Home ✤ Foliage Plants ✤ Flowering Plants ✤ Gift Plants ✤
   Hanging Plants

2. DECORATING WITH PLANTS 22
   Basic Concepts ✤ Decorating Techniques ✤ Preventing Water Damage ✤
   Displaying Plants ✤ Elements of Design ✤ Containers ✤ Form and Mass ✤
   Texture and Scale ✤ Color ✤ Plant Placement ✤ Accent Lighting

3. CHOOSING HOUSEPLANTS 34
   General Considerations ✤ Size of Plants ✤ Shape & Growth Habit ✤
   Characteristic Plant Shapes ✤ Leaf Size & Shape ✤ Leaf & Flower Color ✤
   Buying Plants ✤ Indoor Conditions: Halls and Entryways, Living Rooms and
   Dining Rooms, Bedrooms, Bathrooms, Kitchens ✤ Growing Culinary Herbs Indoors

4. HOUSEPLANT CONTAINERS 50
   Hanging Containers ✤ Pots ✤ Tubs and Urns ✤ Boxes ✤ Choosing Containers ✤
   Pedestals, Stands, Trolleys ✤ How to Install Supports for Hanging Plants

5. RAISING & GROOMING 58
   Basics ✤ Light ✤ Daylengths ✤ Artificial Light ✤ How to Build a Knockdown
   Growing Stand ✤ Soil ✤ Potting ✤ Repotting ✤ Water ✤ Heat and Humidity ✤
   Air Circulation ✤ Fertilizer ✤ Trimming and Grooming ✤ Resting ✤ Seasonal &
   Vacation Care

6. PROPAGATING HOUSEPLANTS 78
   Propagating with Seed ✤ Germinating Seeds ✤ Vegetative Propagation ✤
   Forcing Bulbs for Winter Color ✤ Propagation Methods & Hints

7. PROBLEMS: SYMPTOMS & CURES 96
   Pest and Disease Problems ✤ Poor Care: Symptoms & Possible Causes ✤
   Meet the Insects ✤ Insect Control ✤ Plant Diseases

Part II: Plant Profiles 106

HOW TO READ THE PLANT PROFILES 107

THE PLANTS (ALPHABETICAL BY FAMILY) 108

Glossary 185
Metric Equivalents 186
Index 187
Photo Credits 191

INTRODUCTION

About This Book

Houseplants are beautiful on their own, and well-placed houseplants can transform a room's decor into something extraordinary. Besides their beauty, plants add oxygen and humidity to room air, while also cleansing it by absorbing common household pollutants. And some plants have a lovely fragrance.

In addition, these wonderful life forms possess something akin to personalities. In fact, many indoor gardeners insist that plants respond well to affection and are good listeners. If you've ever observed people caring for houseplants, you may have overheard an exchange resembling an intimate conversation.

Thus, factors of aesthetics and plant nurturing combine to provide profound enjoyment that nourishes the psyche. Indeed, houseplants bless those who tend them, as well as mere onlookers.

ORIGINS & GROWING CONDITIONS

In centuries past, houseplants originated in the wild in various parts of the world. Although many of today's houseplants are pure descendants of their wild parents, countless others have resulted from human matchmaking.

Of the more than 400,000 native plants in the world, houseplants represent a small portion. Although there are more than 35,000 native species of orchids and more than 9,000 ferns, the number of newcomers cultivated by man defies calculation. We present about 200 of the most popular houseplants available in North America.

The featured plant families and groups include traditional houseplants, as well as newcomers, and all are generally available.

People often assume that houseplants come only from tropical climates, where humidity and heat are intense. Although many popular houseplants did originate in the tropics, others evolved in cooler regions. And although many cacti and succulents occur in deserts, others live in tropical rain forests.

Whether growing naturally from wild seed or from one of the many methods of cultivation, houseplants do best in growing conditions similar to those in which their progenitors thrived. Even so, you don't need to transform your home into a jungle or desert to ensure that plants from those climates survive. Most of today's houseplants can adjust to a range of indoor conditions.

Plants can be propagated by various means, including leaf cuttings, as shown here.

How this Book is Structured

Chapter 1 presents the characteristics of the main families and groups from which houseplants come. This first chapter also lists plants profiled in the second part of the book. Chapters 2 through 6 discuss decorating with houseplants, choosing plants and containers, caring for plants, and propagating them by various means. Chapter 7 covers diagnosis and environmentally friendly solutions for plant problems, including diseases and insects.

Part II features photos and descriptions of the most popular plants. For more on using the plant profiles, see page 107.

Principles of plant naming are illustrated in the name Camille dumbcane (*Dieffenbachia picta* 'Camille').

PLANT NAMES

In this book, all plants are listed by common name and scientific (botanical) name. One disadvantage of relying on the common name is that it's not the most reliable way to find the plant you want. This is because many plants are known by more than one common name and because some vastly different plants share a common name.

To ensure accurate identifications, botanists have adopted a world standard for names. They've assigned plants to family trees based mainly on similarities of their reproductive structures. The scientific names are rendered primarily in Latin. So if you know a plant's scientific name, it's easier to obtain the plant you want.

This book employs the scientific names used by the Royal Horticultural Society's *Index of Garden Plants*, as well as older scientific names that are still widely used in houseplant catalogs. When the scientific name has changed, you'll find both the new and old names listed, with one of them noted in parentheses and an "aka," short for "also known as."

When a houseplant has no common name, the scientific name is coined as the common name, such as in guzmania.

Family. In this book, the family is the largest grouping of plants sharing common characteristics. The scientific family name is written with an initial capital letter as in Begoniaceae and is not italicized.

Genus. Normally, the next smaller grouping of plants within a family is the genus, which is written with an initial capital letter and is italicized; the plural for genus is genera. The genus name is usually the first word of a plant's scientific name, as in *Guzmania lingulata*.

Species. The second word in the name indicates species, which is a group of related plants that are alike except for small variations. The species name is italicized.

Variety Vs. Cultivar. Scientists take nomenclature further by assigning a name if the plant is a variety (a variant of a species that occurs as a result of natural mutation) or a cultivar (meaning a *cultivated variety*, resulting from human intervention).

The terms *variety* and *cultivar* are commonly used interchangeably, even though there is a technical difference. A cultivar will be listed with single quotes, (as in the label for the photograph above). When a cultivar is used as part of the common name, as in the example Camille dumbcane, above, single quotes aren't usually used.

Hybrid: A hybrid is a plant that results from the breeding of two genetically different parents. Often written with an ✕, a hybrid may differ in significant ways from its parents and even from its siblings. A hybrid is listed like this: *Begonia* ✕ *hiemalis*.

part
O N E

A World of Plants

1 Foliage, Flowers & Families 10

2 Decorating with Plants 22

3 Choosing Houseplants 34

4 Houseplant Containers 50

5 Raising & Grooming 58

6 Propagating Houseplants 78

7 Problems:
Symptoms & Cures 96

O chapter ONE

Foliage, Flowers & Families

In the past, people could choose from only a small number of houseplants. Various types of philodendrons, parlor palms, African violets, and some ferns were common in most homes, but the selection stopped there. Fortunately, over the years, growers have introduced many new houseplants that grow well. Today, you can choose from literally thousands of plants in all sizes, shapes, and colors. No matter what your design need or growing conditions, you can find a flowering or foliage plant to suit your situation perfectly.

Broadly speaking, there are two categories of houseplants—those prized mainly for their foliage and those valued primarily for their flowers. Within these two categories are plants of every size and description, from miniatures and dwarfs to tree-size specimens, from compact bushes to trailing vines.

The foliage plants include many traditional houseplants.

A corsage orchid elegantly demonstrates why people love to grow flowering plants indoors. Orchids are quite easy to grow.

Their leaves may be deep glossy green, rich emerald, light springlike chartreuse, or combinations of green and other colors. Many foliage plants, like prayer plants (*Calathea*) and dieffenbachias, have variegated, or multicolored, leaves.

Although there are hundreds of foliage plants from which to choose, the realm of flowering plants is even larger and more diverse. Flowering plants offer glamorous color accents that can harmonize with a room's color scheme or add new tones. You can find any color, from the palest pastels to the most vivid reds. Sizes can range from minuscule to large, and forms run the gamut from spiky to daisylike to bell-shaped.

CONDITIONS IN YOUR HOME

Although you'll want houseplants that reflect your personal taste, it's every bit as important to select plants that will fare well in the various growing conditions in your home. For example, certain plants need shade or only moderate light. Others need lots of sun. So the amount of sun and indirect light available in your home dictates to a great extent what you can and cannot grow in each location. In a nutshell, success with houseplants depends largely on your providing the environmental conditions that plants need to thrive.

This wide choice of flowering houseplants includes begonias, orchids, and African violets.

Foliage Plants

Foliage plants are grown primarily for their leaves because they don't bloom under average home conditions, or if they do, the flowers are not showy. Many foliage plants can tolerate low light. For example, philodendrons, snake plant (*Sansevieria*), and cast iron plant (*Aspidistra*) are long-time favorite houseplants because they can survive the dry conditions and low light levels of most homes.

Following are profiles on the families and groups that contain many plants traditionally grown for their foliage, plus listings of family members profiled in Part II of this book.

Known for its unusual foliage, the polka dot plant is a member of the Acanthus family.

Houseplants grown for their foliage display an amazing variety of shapes, textures, and color combinations. Today, you don't need to settle for just Boston ferns and parlor palms.

ACANTHUS FAMILY (ACANTHACEAE)

Although this family contains a number of fine flowering houseplants, including zebra plant (*Aphelandra squarrosa*) and firecracker flower (*Crossandra infundibuliformis*), it is most famous for its foliage plants. The leaves of an acanthus plant inspired the carvings on Corinthian columns. Acanthus family members are found in Mexico, South America, India, Madagascar, and Asia. Especially attractive foliage plants in this family include the polka dot plant (*Hypoestes phyllostachya*) and the striking metallic-purple Persian shield plant (*Strobilanthes dyerianus*). See their profiles on pages 108–111.

Acanthus

❧ Zebra plant, yellow plume plant, (*Aphelandra squarrosa*)
❧ Firecracker flower (*Crossandra infundibuliformis*)
❧ Mosaic plant (*Fittonia verschaffeltii*)
❧ Polka dot plant (*Hypoestes phyllostachya*)
❧ Shrimp plant (*Justicia brandegeana*)
❧ Lollipop plant, yellow shrimp plant (*Pachystachys lutea*)
❧ *Sanchezia speciosa* (*S. nobilis*)
❧ Persian shield plant (*Strobilanthes dyerianus*)

Persian Shield Plant

ARALIA FAMILY (ARALIACEAE)

A diverse group, the Aralia Family includes trees, shrubs, and vines, as well as herbaceous plants (which die back to the ground each winter in their native habitats). Aralias that are popular houseplants include the canopy-like umbrella plant (*Schefflera actinophylla*), which has big, bright green compound leaves that emerge from their stems like fingers on a hand; oriental-looking false aralia (*Dizygotheca*), with its slender serrated leaves; the frilly Balfour aralia (*Polyscias scutellaria* 'Balfourii'), with its small scalloped leaves; and pretty ming aralia (*Polyscias fruticosa*), with leaves that are crinkly and heart-shaped. The familiar English ivy (shown below) is also a member of the Aralia Family, profiled on pages 114–115.

Variegated Umbrella Plant

Aralia

❧ Finger aralia, false aralia (*Dizygotheca elegantissima*)
❧ English ivy (*Hedera helix*)
❧ Ming aralia (*Polyscias fruticosa*)
❧ Balfour aralia (*Polyscias scutellaria* 'Balfourii')
❧ Variegated umbrella plant (*Schefflera actinophylla* 'Variegata')

English Ivy

ARUM FAMILY (ARACEAE)

This diverse family, generally known as the aroids, includes many favorite indoor plants, such as philodendron, anthurium, Chinese evergreen, pothos, alocasia, spathiphyllum, syngonium, and dieffenbachia.

These beautiful foliage plants generally grow in shady, humid locations in South America, near the equator, and in Central America. They come in a range of sizes from small to large, and many varieties have variegated foliage that is splashed, splotched, streaked, or mottled with creamy white, golden yellow, or even red or pink.

Black Velvet Alocasia

Germanic folklore held that arums, particularly philodendrons, brought good luck. But indoor gardeners appreciate the members of this family primarily because they provide beautiful green accents. See their profiles on pages 116–127.

Arum (aka Aroid)

- Chinese evergreen (*Aglaonema* cultivars)
- Shield plant (*Alocasia × amazonica*)
- *Alocasia* 'Black Velvet'
- Copper alocasia (*Alocasia cuprea*)
- Green Goddess alocasia (*Alocasia* 'Green Goddess')
- Tailflower (*Anthurium hookeri*)
- Flamingo flower (*Anthurium scherzerianum*)
- Fancy-leaved caladium (*Caladium × hortulanum*)
- Hilo Beauty colocasia (*Colocasia* 'Hilo Beauty')
- Dumbcane (*Dieffenbachia* species and cultivars)
- Pothos (*Epipremnum* species and cultivars)
- *Homalomena rubescens* 'Emerald Gem'
- Swiss cheese plant (*Monstera deliciosa*)
- *Nephthytis* hybrids

Satin Pothos

- *Philodendron* species and cultivars
- Domino peace lily (*Spathiphyllum* 'Domino')
- White-flag plant (*Spathiphyllum floribundum*)
- Arrowhead plant (*Syngonium podophyllum*)
- Angel's wings (*Xanthosoma lindenii*)
- Calla lily (*Zantedeschia* cultivars)

Camille Dumbcane

FERNS (VARIOUS FAMILIES)

Ferns comprise a group of leafy plants from several botanical families that share the characteristic of reproducing by means of spores instead of seeds; ferns do not bloom with flowers. These lush plants have graced North American homes since Revolutionary times. Most ferns come from shady woodlands and are valued for their divided, often delicate leaves (called *fronds*) and their lush, graceful forms. They offer distinctive leaf shapes ranging from stalk-like (such as those of the cabbage head fern) to fishtail to ruffled (like those of the Boston fern). Some ferns have small, round leaflets, like those of the lovely maidenhair (*Adiantum*) and button (*Pellaea*) ferns. Easy to grow in low light, ferns are outstanding performers indoors. See their profiles on pages 148–151.

Cabbage Head Fern

Ferns

- Lacy maidenhair fern (*Adiantum tenerum*)
- Bird's nest fern (*Asplenium nidus*)
- Tree fern (*Blechnum gibbum*)
- Holly fern (*Cyrtomium falcatum*)
- Japanese shield fern (*Dryopteris erythrosora*)
- Fluffy Ruffles Boston fern (*Nephrolepis exaltata* 'Fluffy Ruffles')
- *Nephrolepis exaltata* 'Timii'
- Button fern (*Pellaea rotundifolia*)
- Cabbage head fern (*Polypodium vulgare*)
- Cretan brake fern (*Pteris cretica*)
- Leather fern (*Rumohra adiantiformis*)

Japanese Shield Fern

Healing Aloe

LILY FAMILY & RELATIVES (LILIACEAE & OTHER FAMILIES)

The large Lily Family is best known for the many kinds of trumpet-shaped flowers grown from bulbs in outdoor gardens and greenhouses. But a surprising number of foliage houseplants, such as spider plant (*Chlorophytum*) and foxtail fern, also belong to the Lily Family. Healing aloe (*Aloe vera*), dracaenas, and cast-iron plant (*Aspidistra*) are also members of this clan. The plants in these families come from several continents—Africa, Australia, and China. See their profiles on pages 158–163.

Lilies & Related Plants
- *Aloe bellatula*
- Healing aloe, medicine plant (*Aloe vera*, aka *A. barbadensis*)
- Foxtail fern (*Asparagus densiflorus* 'Myersii')
- Cast iron plant (*Aspidistra elatior*)
- Bottle plant, ponytail palm (*Beaucarnea recurvata*, aka *Nolina recurvata*)
- Variegated spider plant (*Chlorophytum cosmosum* 'Variegatum')
- Ti plant (*Cordyline terminalis*)
- Dwarf pineapple dracaena (*Dracaena deremensis* 'Compacta')
- Red Wine corn plant (*Dracaena fragrans* 'Red Wine')
- Rainbow dracaena (*Dracaena marginata* 'Tricolor', aka *D. cincta* 'Tricolor')
- Spotted ox tongue plant (*Gasteria bicolor* var. *liliputana*)
- Silver squill (*Ledebouria socialis*)
- Spineless yucca (*Yucca elephantipes*)

MULBERRY FAMILY (MORACEAE)

When you think of the Mulberry Family, you probably think of it as the source of purple tree fruits that birds love or the leaves that were once fed to silkworms to produce the fiber that became the most luxurious of textiles—silk. But some classic foliage houseplants also belong to this family. The handsome ficus, or fig, trees are part of this clan. The diminutive creeping fig (*Ficus pumila*), the graceful weeping fig (*F. benjamina*) in all its variations, and the boldly dramatic braided fig all make excellent houseplants. See their profiles on pages 164–165.

Burgundy Rubber Plant

Mulberries
- Weeping fig, aka banyan tree (*Ficus benjamina*)
- Braided fig (*Ficus benjamina*)
- Variegated fig (*Ficus benjamina* 'Variegata')
- Burgundy rubber plant (*Ficus elastica* 'Burgundy')
- Variegated creeping fig (*Ficus pumila* 'Variegata')

Braided Fig

Spotted Ox Tongue Plant

PALM FAMILY (PALMAE)

Palms were a symbol of riches in ancient cultures. Considered sacred to Apollo, palms were said to have been introduced to Greece by Hercules. During the 1800s, palms were fixtures in parlors and conservatories, but they eventually fell out of favor. They were later grown mainly as outdoor plants in warm climates. But palms are again becoming popular as indoor plants, and with good reason. They are generally undemanding, and many do well in low light. Notable examples include lady palm and bamboo palm. A large, leafy palm can be a striking presence. See their profiles on pages 172–173.

Palms

- Fishtail palm (*Caryota mitis*)
- Bamboo palm (*Chamaedorea erumpens*)
- Butterfly palm (*Chrysalidocarpus lutescens*)
- Chinese fan palm (*Licuala grandis*)
- Lady palm (*Rhapis excelsa*)

SPIDERWORT FAMILY (COMMELINACEAE)

The Spiderwort Family is the source of some favorite houseplants. Generally having smooth, pointed leaves, the plants often have a trailing habit, as exemplified by the basket plants known as wandering Jew (*Zebrina* and *Callisia* genera). Some family members have green foliage, but the leaves of others are colored purple or bronze, or striped in silver, green, purple, and even pink. Spiderworts rarely bloom indoors, but some will flower if given bright sun from a southern exposure. See their profiles on pages 174–175.

Purple Heart Plant

Spiderwort

- Brazilian wandering Jew (*Callisia repens*)
- Moses-in-a-boat (*Rhoeo spathacea*)
- Purple heart plant (*Setcreasea pallida*, aka *Tradescantia pallida*)
- Wandering Jew (*Zebrina pendula*)

Butterfly Palm

Chinese Fan Palm

Brazilian Wandering Jew

Kaffir Lily

Flowering Plants

Most plants flower, but the plants grown primarily for their showy flowers are the ones we call flowering plants. In the past, most flowering plants were grown mainly in greenhouses and conservatories because they generally demanded more sunlight and more humidity than the average home could

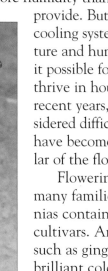

Crown-of-Thorns

provide. But newer home heating and cooling systems, with better temperature and humidity control, have made it possible for more flowering plants to thrive in houses and apartments. In recent years, even orchids—long considered difficult to grow in homes— have become some of the most popular of the flowering houseplants.

Flowering houseplants come from many families. Gesneriads and begonias contain hundreds of available cultivars. And exotic plant families such as gingers and bromeliads bring brilliant color into the home.

Two other huge "groups" of plants that bloom indoors are cacti and succulents. These groups are usually lumped together because they generally grow well in arid conditions, although some cacti are native to jungle habitats and need more moisture than their desert-dwelling relatives. Succulent plants are able to store water in their tissues. Both groups include plants that are grown for flowers as well as foliage, including the crown-of-thorns, orchid cactus, and ever-popular Christmas cactus.

AMARYLLIS FAMILY (AMARYLLIDACEAE)

The plants in this family grow from bulbs or corms, and most come from South Africa, the Mediterranean area, or South America. Many lovely houseplants belong to this clan, including amaryllis (*Hippeastrum*), fireball (*Haemanthus*, aka *Scadoxus*), Amazon lily (*Eucharis*), and kaffir lily (*Clivia*). These plants are related to the Lily Family, as their trumpet-shaped flowers attest. Plants in this family also have long,

strap-shaped leaves. After blooming, these plants need a rest period before they will flower again. See their profiles on pages 112–113.

Amaryllis
- Kaffir lily (*Clivia miniata*)
- Amazon lily (*Eucharis* × *grandiflora*)
- Fireball, Catherine wheel (*Haemanthus katherinae*, *Scadoxus multiflorus* ssp. *katherinae*)
- Amaryllis (*Hippeastrum* cultivars)

BEGONIA FAMILY (BEGONIACEAE)

This enormous family consisting of one genus from South America contains thousands of species and cultivars, ranging in size from a few inches to several feet tall.

Begonias are divided into groups of plants based on appearance and growth habit. This book organizes the genus into five major groups, as follows:

Angel-wing begonias are mainly fibrous rooted, with cane-like stems that may stand up straight or cascade when grown in a hanging basket. The leaves are wing-shaped, with one lobe larger than the other. Leaf colors range from apple green to greenish brown with dots and spots of silver or white. Flowers in shades of pink, red, salmon, and orange bloom mainly in spring and summer.

Hirsute (meaning hairy-leaved) begonias have leaves flecked with short hairs. Their bearded flowers are white or greenish white to pink. Blooming times vary but occur mainly in fall and winter.

Rhizomatous begonias may have round or star-shaped leaves that range in color from plain green to variegated in fancy patterns. The rhizomes store moisture for the plants.

Semperflorens (meaning everblooming), or wax begonias, are compact plants with small glossy leaves that may be solid green, variegated with creamy white, or reddish bronze in color. They bear small flowers in many warm colors.

Rex begonias are grown exclusively for their patterned foliage that shimmers in combinations of silver, metallic green, and purple. Hundreds of cultivars are available. Rex means "king," and many of these plants are so exquisite they are fit for royalty. See their profiles on pages 128–131.

Begonias

- *Begonia* 'Cleopatra'
- Reiger begonia (*Begonia* × *hiemalis*)
- *Begonia* 'Kewensis'
- Red-leaf begonia (*Begonia* hybrid)
- Angel-wing begonia (*Begonia* hybrids)
- *Begonia* 'Picotee'
- Rex begonia (*Begonia* Rex-Cultorum hybrids)
- Wax begonia (*Begonia* Semperflorens-Cultorum hybrids)
- Maple-leaf begonia (*Begonia superba* 'Rana')

Picotee Begonia

BROMELIAD FAMILY (BROMELIACEAE)

Perhaps best known for one family member, the pineapple, bromeliads are beginning to rival orchids in popularity. There are more than 2,000 species, both terrestrial and epiphytic (growing in trees), mainly from South American rain forests. Bromeliads are prized for their colorful bracts, which come in shades of red, rose, orange, yellow, purple, and pink-blushed white, and for their exquisite foliage, which may be banded, striped, or splashed in combinations of green, silver, pink, red, purple, yellow, black, or cream. Bromeliads are nearly indestructible. See their profiles on pages 132–139.

Aechmea chantinii

Bromeliads

- Silver urn plant (*Aechmea chantinii* hybrid)
- Urn plant (*Aechmea fasciata*)
- Variegated pineapple plant (*Ananas cosmosus* 'Variegatus')
- Fantasia bromeliad (*Billbergia* 'Fantasia')
- Earth star (*Cryptanthus* species and hybrids)
- *Guzmania lingulata* 'Orange Star'
- *Guzmania lingulata* 'Rana'
- Poker plant (*Guzmania zahnii*)
- Striped neoregelia (*Neoregelia carolinae* forma *tricolor*)
- *Neoregelia* 'Royal Burgundy'
- Blushing bromeliad (*Neoregelia* hybrid)
- Fingernail plant (*Neoregelia spectabilis*)
- Plume bromeliad (*Tillandsia cyanea*)
- Tufted bromeliad (*Tillandsia ionantha*)
- Yellow poker plant (*Vriesea* hybrid)
- Flaming sword (*Vriesea* × *poelmanii*, *Vriesea splendens*)

'Orange Star' Bromeliad

Yellow Poker Plant

CACTUS FAMILY (CACTACEAE) & SUCCULENTS (VARIOUS FAMILIES)

All cacti are succulents, which are plants with swollen fleshy leaves and stems that can hold water for long periods. Even though all cacti are succulents, not all succulents are cacti. Even so, catalogs and retail outlets tend to group cacti with other succulents. Usually thought of as desert plants, many cacti—such as the Christmas cactus (*Schlumbergera* × *buckleyi*)—live in rain forests. They require almost as much water as other plants, although many are accustomed to dry dormant periods when little or no rain falls in their natural habitats. See their profiles on pages 140–146.

Torch Cactus

Cacti and Succulents

- Desert rose (*Adenium obesum*)
- Peanut cactus (*Chamaecereus sylvestrii*, aka *Echinopsis chamaecereus*)
- Jade tree (*Crassula ovata*, aka *C. argentea*)
- False rose (*Echeveria* hybrid)
- Crown-of-thorns (*Euphorbia milii*)
- Wax plant, porcelain flower (*Hoya carnosa*)
- Felt bush, velvet leaf (*Kalanchoe beharensis*)
- Starfire kalanchoe (*Kalanchoe blossfeldiana*)
- Dinner-plate kalanchoe (*Kalanchoe thyrsiflora*)
- Globe cactus (*Mammillaria celsiana*, aka *M. muehlenpfordtii*)
- *Pachyphytum* species
- Ball cactus (*Parodia penicillata*)
- Easter cactus (*Rhipsalidopsis rosea*, *Hatiora rosea*)
- Pencil cactus (*Rhipsalis* species)
- Christmas cactus (*Schlumbergera* × *buckleyi*)
- Thanksgiving cactus (*Schlumbergera truncata*)
- Donkey's tail (*Sedum morganianum*)
- Starfish flower (*Stapelia gigantea*)
- Torch cactus (*Trichocereus candicans*, aka *Echinocereus candicans*)

Easter Cactus

Poinsettia

EUPHORBIA FAMILY (EUPHORBIACEAE)

This is one of the world's most diverse plant families. Its members range widely in appearance and include spiny succulents, flowering plants, and plants grown primarily for their colorful foliage. All members of this family have a sticky white sap that bleeds out when the plants are cut. This sap can irritate human skin and eyes upon contact, so wear gloves when pruning the plants. One of the most popular euphorbias is the poinsettia, which is now available with white, pink or two-tone leaves. See their profiles on page 147.

Euphorbias

- Chenille plant (*Acalypha hispida*)
- Croton (*Codiaeum variegatum* var. *pictum*)
- Poinsettia (*Euphorbia pulcherrima*)

GESNERIAD FAMILY (GESNERIACEAE)

Gesneriads come mainly from South America; some family members are from Africa. Most Gesneriads have flowers that provide vivid fall and winter color. And some, such as Cape primrose and African violet, flower for much of the year. The African violet is available in many sizes, from miniature to dwarf to standard, and it blooms in shades of purple, blue-violet, pink, and deep red, as well as white. The flowers may be single, double, star-shaped, fringed, or edged in white. Family members too often overlooked include the flame violet (*Episcia*), with its ornamental foliage and brilliant red flowers; the goldfish plant (*Nematanthus*), which bears small orange flowers that look like tiny goldfish;

Gloxinia

the Cape primrose (*Streptocarpus*), with clusters of pretty tubular blossoms; and columneas, trailing plants with flowers in shades of yellow and orange. See their profiles on pages 152–155.

Gesneriads
- Lipstick plant (*Aeschynanthus* species)
- Button columnea (*Columnea arguta*)
- Flame violet (*Episcia cupreata*)
- Goldfish plant (*Nematanthus gregarius*, aka *Hypocyrta nummularia*)
- African violet (*Saintpaulia* cultivars)
- Gloxinia (*Sinningia* hybrids)
- Temple bells (*Smithiantha speciosus*)
- Cape primrose and *Streptocarpella* Cape primrose (*Streptocarpus* hybrids)

GINGER FAMILY (ZINGIBERACEAE)
From Malaysia and India, gingers have only recently become popular houseplants. Butterfly ginger (*Globba*), resurrection lily (*Kaempferia*), and several other members of the Ginger Family are adding their tropical elegance to more and more interiors. These striking plants have elongated leaves and spikes of fragrant flowers in warm shades of yellow, gold, apricot, orange, coral, red, pink, and white. With their unusual and stunning color, they create a bright ambiance. See their profiles on pages 156–157.

Gingers
- Orange tulip (*Costus curvibracteatus*)
- Crepe paper flower (*Costus cuspidatus*)
- Siam tulip (*Curcuma alismatifolia*)
- Java tulip (*Curcuma* species)
- Butterfly ginger (*Globba winitti*)
- Resurrection lily (*Kaempferia rotunda*)

Crepe Paper Flower

ORCHID FAMILY (ORCHIDACEAE)
In the wild, orchids inhabit almost every corner of the globe. There are at least 35,000 wild species. In North America, orchids are the top-selling houseplants. With retail sales exceeding $100 million per year, they have surpassed even African violets in popularity. The plants are enjoyed as houseplants both because they are beautiful and because they can tolerate neglect. The flowers of many orchid genera, such as *Oncidium*, *Cattleya*, and *Phalaenopsis*, last for weeks or even months. Orchids offer a dazzling array of flower forms, sizes, and colors. Some are fragrant as well. Given the right growing conditions, orchids bloom reliably year after year. See their profiles on pages 166–171.

Orange Cattleya Orchid

Orchids
- Stefan Isler orchid (× *Burrageara* 'Stefan Isler')
- Guatemalan orchid (*Cattleya guatemalensis*)
- Corsage flower (*Cattleya* hybrid)
- Wildcat orchid (× *Colmanara* 'Wildcat')
- Jill Katalinca orchid (*Cymbidium* 'Jill Katalinca')
- Stars 'n' Bars orchid (× *Degarmoara* 'Stars 'n' Bars')
- Antelope orchid (*Dendrobium antennatum*)
- Topaz dendrobium (*Dendrobium bullenianum*)
- *Epidendrum stamfordianum*
- Dancing lady orchid (*Oncidium maculatum* 'Paolo')
- Sharry Baby orchid (*Oncidium* 'Sharry Baby')
- Lady slipper orchid (*Paphiopedilum insigne*)
- Red Sky lady slipper orchid (*Paphiopedilum* 'Red Sky')
- Lady slipper orchid (*Paphiopedilum sukhakulii*)
- Moth orchid, dogwood orchid (*Phalaenopsis* hybrids)
- Orange cattleya (*Sophrolaeliocattleya* Hazel Boyd 'Sunset')
- Winter orchid (*Zygopetalum crinitum*)

Stars 'n' Bars Orchid

Hydrangea

❧ Gift Plants ❧

Although gift plants come from many different plant families, they have become so closely associated with holiday and seasonal giving, they deserve their own category. At Christmas, the most popular gift plants include Christmas cactus (page 145) and poinsettia (page 147). Next come Easter cactus (page 144) and Easter lilies.

Gardenias are especially popular for Mother's Day. Greenhouse growers force hydrangeas into bloom for sale in spring. Elegant calla lilies (page 127) are widely available in spring and summer.

There are many plants, including chrysanthemum, Thanksgiving cactus (page 145), amaryllis (pages 112–113), and florist's cyclamen (page 183), that thrive in the cool autumn weather. Available throughout the year, gloxinias (page 154), are especially nice in winter and spring. And there are orchid cultivars in bloom almost every month (pages 166–171).

To make gift plants last, keep the soil moderately moist, but do not fertilize. Keep the plants in dappled sunlight, and maintain moderate temperatures. Keep daytime temperatures no higher than 78°F because heat quickly desiccates these plants. Pick off dead leaves and flowers as soon as you notice them.

Keeping Gift Plants Growing. Unfortunately, it is difficult or impossible to get many gift plants, including chrysanthemums and hydrangeas, to grow well or rebloom indoors, so they are not profiled in Part II of this book. Enjoy them while they are blooming, but discard them when they are finished.

Other gift plants can be grown as houseplants. Bulbous plants, such as cyclamen, can be kept, as can nonbulbous orchids and Christmas cactus.

When bulbous plants finish blooming, repot and grow them in fresh soil as you would other houseplants. Stop watering bulbous plants when the foliage dies. Then unpot the bulbs, and store them in a cool, dry, dim place for six to eight weeks. Then replant the bulbs in fresh soil, and water only sparingly. You'll soon see new growth, at which time you can water to keep the soil evenly moist. If all goes well, a new crop of flowers will appear.

*Cape Jasmine
Gardenia*

Easter Lily

Chrysanthemum

Cyclamen

Plants trailing from hanging baskets are popular, and it's easy to see why. Hanging plants with cascading leaves and flowers look graceful and draw

the eye. Today there are many kinds of containers available for hanging plants. The lavish growth and handsome foliage of new varieties of favorites such as pothos (page 121) make it easy to create a lush, plant-filled paradise in your home. The wax plant (page 141), a popular old-fashioned vine, is now available in many cultivars. Some have striped or mottled leaves, and the clusters of waxy white or pink flowers are sweetly fragrant—a cherished asset in a home.

Trailing angel-wing begonias (page 130) are resplendent with color. They have lovely, silver-

Goldfish Plant

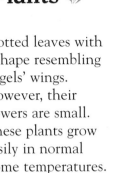

spotted leaves with a shape resembling angels' wings. However, their flowers are small. These plants grow easily in normal home temperatures.

Lipstick Plant

The Gesneriad family presents fine red-flowering lipstick plants (page 152) and the aptly named goldfish plant (page 153), with puffy orange blossoms. Another relative, the columnea (page 152), is dainty and pretty.

For best results, choose a container that has an attached saucer so that you can water without fear of damaging floors and furniture. (See pages 50–51 for detailed information on these containers.)

Also, examine the hanging device, usually a wire or plastic hook, to ensure that it is sturdy enough to support the weight of the basket. Most important, install ceiling or wall hardware securely enough to support the weight. Hanging baskets full of damp soil can be quite heavy and make an awful mess when they come crashing down. See pages 56–57 for guidance on hanging containers securely. For a more complete list of trailing plants, see "Plants for Hanging Containers," on page 51. For more information on caring for specific kinds on hanging plants, consult Part II of this book, beginning on page 108.

Swedish Ivy

Button Columnea

chapter
TWO

Decorating with Plants

Houseplants can be an important component of room decor and can even transform a home into an indoor garden. They can enhance the overall ambiance, cleanse the air, and provide visual accents and focal points. Imparting a garden-like setting, houseplants also can give solace and brighten your spirits.

You can place your houseplants for different purposes: decorating windows, adorning table-tops, creating cascades from hanging containers, hiding unattractive walls, and enlivening plain interiors. Large plants can serve as screens, room dividers, or other architectural elements.

Windows are logical locations for houseplants because they let in the light that plants need to

Houseplants add color and style to an ordinary table. Shown here is a mix of flowering and foliage plants including orchids, ferns, and alocasias.

Bring the outdoors inside with an arrangement of potted plants. The vertical cactus anchors the scene and adds drama, while the varied leaf shapes of the other plants provide eye-catching texture.

This window greenhouse results in a rainbow of color. Shown here are coleus, cyclamen, and begonia.

Houseplants dress up a plain corner: Railings and furniture combine to create visual boundaries.

grow. Whether on shelves, on windowsills, or in hanging containers in front of windows, houseplants soften hard, structural lines and provide welcome texture and color. You can position large plants on either side of a window to frame an attractive view—or hang basket plants at different levels before a window to create a living screen rather than resorting to curtains or blinds. Even skylights can admit enough light for some plants to grow.

DECORATING TECHNIQUES

Use houseplants that will draw and hold the viewer's attention. Your goal should be a pleasing composition that contributes to the style of the room, not a haphazardly arranged jungle. Orchids, angel-wing begonias, and episcias are some of the many good sun-loving plants for a position near a window or below a skylight.

Another technique employs plants to create a transition between an indoor room and the outdoors. If you have sliding glass doors or a large bay window, place houseplants inside that resemble—or are related to—plants growing outdoors.

This outdoor garden room springs to life with plants that thrive in sunny locations. Some of the plants here that thrive in diffused, sunny locations include gingers and orchids.

In the Southwest, for example, an outdoor garden could be echoed by potted cacti and succulents indoors. In the Southeast, palms and gingers can create a continuous tropical feeling, both indoors and out.

PREVENTING WATER DAMAGE

It can be a challenge to prevent water from dripping onto woodwork and floors when you water houseplants close to windows. To avoid damage, either place plants over flooring impervious to water (such as tile), carry plants to a sink to water them, put waterproof saucers under the plant containers, or use containers that have attached saucers. Water the plants slowly so that the water doesn't spill over the container edges and is not too much for the saucers to handle.

Another option is to place pots atop a layer of pebbles in cachepots, most of which do not have drainage holes. Cachepots are decorative pots that hold a plain pot in which a plant is actually potted. The pebbles prevent the bottom of the inner pot from staying constantly wet, thereby helping prevent root rot. Be sure that the drainage water

This tropical oasis includes simple elements: a white chair and shades, and houseplants that contrast with them.

in the cachepot does not rise higher than the pebbles and flood the inner pot.

DISPLAYING PLANTS

You can display houseplants in myriad ways for special effects. A single specimen on a table or mantel will add a burst of welcome color. You can group plants on shelves or racks, or turn a favorite specimen into a focal point by displaying it on a stand or pedestal.

Houseplants can make dim corners inviting, especially when you place them in attractive ceramic containers or on stands. Orchids and gesneriads displayed this way are particularly breathtaking. In fact, they can be more striking than traditional cut flowers, and they usually last much longer.

With adequate lighting, larger plants can fill unused corners or stand near a chair or couch to bring the outdoors into the room, lending a green feeling. Large houseplants mounted on dollies can be moved about according to whim, perhaps positioned to frame a doorway or to serve as a green sculpture or accent in a room. And a large spotlit specimen plant can be a dramatic focal point.

Displaying plants: This gloxinia's bright red flowers and glossy green leaves shout for attention when situated near these cobalt blue glasses. An asparagus fern, at left, softens the edges in this bold tableau.

Practically every room in the house offers places for plants, as shown later in this chapter. Even kitchens and bathrooms can be decorated with houseplants. In fact, these rooms tend to have good light and humidity, two elements on which most houseplants thrive. In the kitchen, houseplants lend a cozy feeling. And plants in bathrooms soften what otherwise tend to be hard-edged, utilitarian lines.

Elements of Design

As with antiques and artwork, you will get the greatest impact from houseplants if you arrange them according to established aesthetic principles. Balance, proportion, and harmony are important. One houseplant in a room can look lonely and out of place, but a well-balanced grouping of three or five plants can become a synchronized team in harmony with its surroundings. Similarly, a 5-foot dieffenbachia on one side of a room and a 5-inch begonia on the other side

When grouping small plants, use different heights to promote interest. The poinsettia on the floor anchors the stage for the angel's wings.

would be out of balance, but repeating these same plants together in other areas of the room can create a sense of rhythm and proportion.

Try to give some thought to plant arrangements, placing them with the same amount of care as you would furniture. (See "Plant Placement," page 31, for more details.) After choosing locations for your plants, stand back and survey the overall arrangement. Does the picture say what you want it to? If not, keep moving and arranging plants until you achieve the desired effect.

Classic elements of design are at work in the range of sizes and textures in this eclectic room. Some of the plants here include ferns, bromeliads, and dracaena.

Grouping small plants. Smaller plants gain visual impact when you group several together. When grouping plants, aim for a variety of sizes and a range of textures. Arrange the plants so the change in height or texture is gradual, rather than placing the smallest plant next to the tallest one or placing the boldest, coarsest plant next to one with the smallest, most delicate leaves. Also, try to create some depth. Set some pots in front and others in back, instead of lining them up like a row of soldiers.

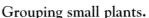

Form and mass here create a balanced display. Shown left to right are a vertical fig, a bushy fern, and—for accent— an amaryllis.

The flowering tuberous begonia—always elegant—looks at home atop this ornate table pedestal.

CONTAINERS

A well-chosen container displays the plant to its best advantage and becomes a decorating element. Select containers that are in proportion to the plants they display. Also, the texture of the plants should be compatible with nearby plants and with the room's decor. For example, a cachepot looks more formal than a wicker basket, and a terra-cotta pot looks more natural than a colored plastic pot. When in doubt, it's always safe to use a white ceramic pot, which complements almost any decor and houseplant.

Consider, too, that extra height adds to the importance and grace of a houseplant. Most houseplants look best when elevated slightly, on a dolly or display stand. Even a saucer can give a plant a little lift.

See Chapter 4, beginning on page 50, for detailed information on the types of containers available for houseplants.

FORM AND MASS

One of the most important design qualities of a houseplant is its *form*, or shape. For example, plants such as schefflera often have a canopy-shape. Other plants may appear fountainlike, rounded, rosette-shaped, or trailing. Leaves can be oval, round, elliptical, lance-shaped, straplike, or delicate and feathery. You can achieve spectacular results if you use one form to echo another in a room—by placing a tall, arching palm in front of a tall, arching window, for example.

Yet a contrast of dissimilar forms can be equally pleasing, such as a columnar cactus against the horizontal lines of walls and furnishings. You need to decide where and when you want such accents. Tall, columnar houseplants can serve as bold sculptures—aralias (*Polyscias*) are among the best plants for this effect. Other good vertical plants include palms, dieffenbachias, tall dracaenas, weeping fig, and columnar cacti.

A group of forms or shapes creates *mass*, another important aspect of design. Masses of low, bushy plants look best softening the hard edges of furniture. For this, ferns are ideal low-growing plants, as are calatheas, orchids, and Chinese evergreens (*Aglaonema* species), especially when set off by beautiful plant stands or pedestals, as shown on the previous page.

Columnar plants, such as these cacti (right), add sculptural accents and a Southwestern look to this room.

❧ Plant Forms ❧

Canopylike

Spreading to Fountainlike

Rosette-Shaped

Treelike

Trailing

A few fine-textured plants unite this room. The plants are in scale with their settings, from the tall tree in the corner to the short, bushy plants near the chairs. Note the trailers atop the cupboards.

Scale. The scale of plants in relation to one another and to the room must be appropriate. Visualize an overgrown palm stooped against an 8-foot-high ceiling. The bent plant, searching for light, would look restricted and awkward and make the whole room feel uncomfortable. Similarly, a small African violet on a grand piano would become lost in the piano's mass.

COLOR

Houseplant colors can affect a room's personality. Color perception is determined by the light that strikes and reflects from surfaces or is absorbed by them. Each color has *value*, that is, lightness or darkness. Also, a color can be warm, such as red, or cool, such as blue.

TEXTURE AND SCALE

Texture describes the surface quality and visual weight of a plant. *Scale* is the relationship of one object to another. When these two qualities are well considered, houseplants can greatly enhance a room's decor.

Texture. Plants considered to be coarse-textured have bolder leaves and more dramatic proportions. Fine-textured plants have small, delicate leaves and slender stems.

You can use texture and scale to change the perception of space in a room. For example, a fine-textured plant such as a small-leaved creeping fig (*Ficus pumila*) positioned at the far end of a room will fool the eye as you enter, creating the illusion that the plant is farther away, making the room seem larger. On the other hand, placing a bold, large-leaved plant at the far end of the room can help make the space look smaller, more intimate, and more inviting.

Color and Light. Houseplants are seen in either natural daylight or in artificial light. The type and quality of that light affect how colors are perceived. Sunlight from a southern window appears warmer than the cool light entering a

Leaf textures of various houseplants include (left to right) begonia, pilea, and plectranthus.

Colorful indoor flowering bulb gardens create an early spring. Narcissus, crocus, tulips, and muscari bloom here.

The color of foliage appears to change in different light. The leaves of this Chinese evergreen are beautifully highlighted in the afternoon sun.

north window. Day and night also affect color perception, and so do the different types of artificial light. For example, incandescent lamps cast a warmer light than fluorescents.

First, you need to decide what times of day are most important for viewing your plants. Determine whether your rooms are visually warm or cool at those times, before you consider the colors and color values of your houseplants. For example, a plant is not just green. It may be dark green, like the leaves of a rubber plant, or light green, like the fronds of

This color wheel, made of a sampling of the many colors of houseplant foliage and flowers, demonstrates that nature starts with the primary colors of yellow, red, and blue, and combines them for endless variations. Colors opposite one another are complementary. Neighboring hues tend to harmonize.

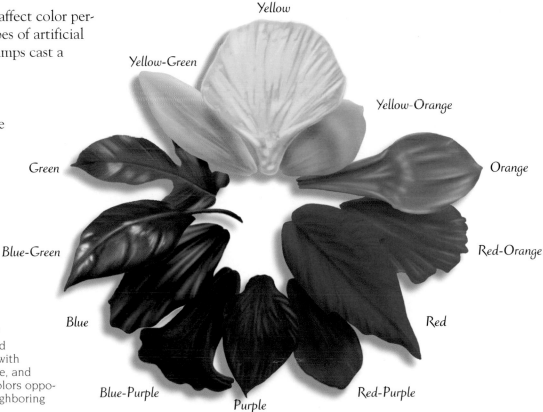

Yellow

Yellow-Green

Yellow-Orange

Green

Orange

Blue-Green

Red-Orange

Blue

Red

Blue-Purple

Red-Purple

Purple

A mass of texture and color can be created by grouping foliage and flowering plants together. Shown here are mosaic plant, poinsettia, begonia, and arrowhead plant.

Color differences exist even among cultivars of the same plant, as illustrated by these crotons. Some are green, others variegated. With so much choice in plants today, you can choose colors that harmonize with the room.

a lacy maidenhair fern. Also, the rubber plant's leaves are leathery and almost opaque, allowing no light to pass through the leaves. So the plant appears dark and heavy. On the other hand, the delicate fronds of the lacy maidenhair fern allow light to pass through them, giving the plant a pale, airy look.

Beyond Green. Colors besides green are important too. Variegated leaves are marked or margined with a color other than green. And flowering plants also contribute color. When adding plants to your decor, choose colors that echo, harmonize with, or contrast with the colors in the room. If your furnishings are of darker wood tones, use dark-valued plants—dark green, purple-green, and blue-green—to create a harmonious look of dark on dark. A burgundy rubber plant (*Ficus elastica* 'Burgundy') or a multicolored maranta would be a good choice. Then you could create dramatic contrast by adding a few light green plants, with yellow-green or apple green foliage, or variegated plants, such as dracaena or coleus. Refer to the color wheel on the previous page for a visual example of complementary colors.

The airy, yellow flowers of this orchid stand out against the deep red wall, providing subtle pyrotechnics against dark walls and lightening weight of the heavy furniture.

Plant Placement

Considering basic design elements, you can use plants to bring out the latent beauty of a room. The living room is usually the most formal room in a home, and often it's also the largest space. So a living room tastefully decorated sets a tone for your house. However, if your living room contains only furniture, the room can lack warmth and impact. Plants, with their color variations, personality, and character add a dimension of vigor, color, and texture.

Here's an illustration of the basic principles of designing with plants: Consider the usual rectangular shape of most living rooms. The sofa, which is usually the starting point for the positioning of other furniture, is one large mass.

The sofa is usually placed against a long wall because the wall can handle the sofa's mass. But suppose the sofa or sofas were instead perpendicular to the wall, far enough from the wall to allow space for an end table or two with a lamp on one end and a passageway on the other. To balance the mass of the sofa, you could place next to it a large plant or several smaller ones or even mass the plants. Such an arrangement could provide contrasts in texture and value—and enhance balance as well.

Matching Plants to Rooms. When choosing plants and their locations, try to match the visual mass and weight of plants to the size and proportion of the room. For example, it's usually better

Correct plant placement, using balance, form, and texture, is represented in this living room. The fig tree in the corner sets the stage for the other plants, which accentuate, rather than compete with, the green upholstery.

Plants of diverse sizes and shapes fill this corner. The plants shown include philodendron (trained up the post) and a palm. The basket pot jackets add texture and mass.

This horizontally trained trailing plant draws attention to the wood trim without obscuring it. The plant's position in the corner softens the hard lines.

to use bigger, bolder plants in a large room. Also, group plants of different sizes to create visual interest. For added height, try placing a small plant on a plant stand or pedestal behind a larger plant on the floor. If you have a number of smaller plants, place them on shelves or on a tiered plant stand to create greater impact.

Symmetrical, well-trained plants with large, smooth-textured leaves, such as *Dieffenbachia amoena* and corn plant (*Dracaena fragrans* 'Massangeana'), are highly appropriate for formal rooms. They are often best centrally positioned in front of a large window and become an important design element when repeated. In a large, open, L-shaped room, consider the space carefully, and try to imagine groups of plants from all sides. If the room has beams or cornices that make strong horizontal lines, consider a row of plants to carry through the horizontal motif. Rooms with slanted

Different-height plants with similar texture are here combined effectively. The ceramic pedestal on the left elevates the plant and brings the lovely pot nearer eye level, while its dark base recedes into the background.

An island of green, such as this collection of ferns on the floor, can divide a large space. The feathery plants atop the walls echo the theme and expand the exhibit.

or hipped ceilings look best with groups of plants. If the ceiling is vaulted or cathedral-shaped, you can plant cascading or fountainlike plants such as philodendrons or arching palms in hanging baskets to create a harmonious look.

Accent Lighting

Today, you have many options for accent lighting with attractive, easy-to-install fixtures. Lamp manufacturers and home-improvement centers offer many accent lamps—both floodlights and spotlights—specifically designed to feature plants and to help them grow indoors.

Floodlights are most suitable for accents because they can light almost the entire plant. With floodlights there is no sharply focused beam pattern. Instead, the most intense light is at the

Track lighting allows you to move fixtures into positions to spotlight plants as needed. The full length of the tracks are electrified, allowing you maximum flexibility to move the fixtures and your plants to your liking.

outer limits, and the illumination drops 10 percent of the maximum at the center of the beam. For information on growing plants under artificial light, see Chapter 5, pages 56–61.

Track lighting has evolved as well. The track is a strip of hardware mounted on a ceiling or wall. You can attach contemporary lamp fixtures to the track at any given point and angle them in various directions. Display-lighting tracks can be used in straight lines or in various patterns to cover almost any desired plant or portion of it.

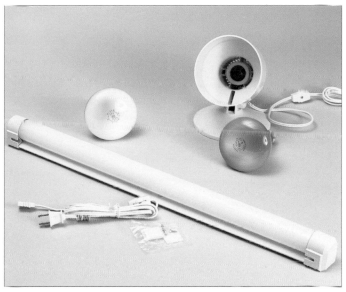

This assortment of plant lights (shown clockwise from top) includes a floodlight fixture with a blue grow-light bulb, a fluorescent tube, and an accent floodlight bulb.

chapter THREE

Choosing Houseplants

Many people buy houseplants on impulse, choosing in a moment's fancy. Yet when selecting plants, it's wise to consider their future as well. For example, consider a plant's growth habit and its eventual size and colors. Some plants look far different young than they do when mature. Some become slender and graceful. Some begin to cascade. Others develop a broad, bushy habit.

Young and mature plants can be displayed using a tiered plant stand. As plants grow, they can be moved to different shelves.

Without the gracefully mature palm at right and the compact fern in the next room, this room setting would lose much of its charm.

Tall, imposing plants can benefit high-ceilinged living spaces. The plants visually lower the ceiling and divide the open space, changing a utilitarian space into inviting living quarters.

Size of Plants

Most rooms have space for at least two plants, but not every room has space for two *large* plants. Large, treelike houseplants grow 4 to 8 feet tall. In retail outlets, these larger plants are often called *specimen* (or *select*) plants, meaning that they are already mature and at the peak of their form. Specimen plants can cost $150 or more.

Medium-size plants generally cost $15 to $25. If your space and money are limited, you can buy medium-size plants and treat them as specimens by elevating them on pedestals or tables. Small plants in 6-inch pots can be suitable, too, and allow you the joy of watching them grow and mature over time. These small plants are usually classified as *starter plants*. Usually neither too large nor too small for most rooms, small plants are good choices for beginners.

Caution: Beginners should avoid plants in 2-, 3-, or 4-inch pots, because these are just past the seedling stage and are not yet strong. To survive, such seedlings need more care and coddling than plants well established in larger pots.

Also, plants can remain small (to 18 inches), or become medium size (19 to 36 inches), or large (taller than 36 inches). And foliage can become almost any shade of green or perhaps reddish, golden, purple, or variegated (with two or more colors).

Also consider a plant's needs in relation to the environmental conditions in your home. Some plants require lots of sun; others prefer dappled light; and still others tolerate shade or dim light. Some won't tolerate drafts or nighttime temperatures below 55°F. (See the plant profiles, beginning on page 108, for information on the needs of individual plants.)

Before you buy, try to locate a garden center, nursery, or other source that supplies high-quality plants. And no matter where you buy, examine each plant carefully for problems, as discussed on page 41.

Small- and medium-size plants at all levels provide a cheery note of welcome in this sunny entryway—without blocking traffic.

Shape & Growth Habit

Again, some young plants look far different from the way they will look when fully mature. Dragon tree (*Dracaena concinna*, aka *D. marginata*) when young has one or two nondescript branches. But at maturity, dragon tree bears large, thrusting branches, each crowned with a cluster of dramatic-looking, red-edged spear-shaped leaves. Butterfly palm (*Chrysalidocarpus lutescens*) grows into a fountain shape. Lady palm (*Rhapis excelsa*) stays low as it matures but becomes bushier. When young, bamboo palm (*Chamaedorea erumpens*) is a slender stalklike plant; it becomes somewhat bushy at maturity.

The characteristic growth pattern of a plant is called its habit. Houseplant habits are generally classified as shrublike, treelike, fountain-shaped, canopylike, rosette-shaped, or cascading. For the best visual effect in a room, try to select plants with lines that will contrast with the dominant lines of the room. Thus, to soften the hard lines of a room, use fountain-shaped or canopylike plants. Or if you prefer, exaggerate the linear space of such a room using large, vertical, treelike plants. Of course, always keep in mind your home's space restrictions. Avoid overwhelming a room with too many plants or with specimens that are too large for it. Otherwise, the space will feel crowded, even junglelike.

This trailing succulent will never outgrow its space alongside the stairway, where it diverts attention from otherwise uninspiring structural elements.

The vertical sansevieria breaks up the strong horizontal lines of the fireplace. The caladium adds balance and stretches the scene while focusing attention on the hearth.

❦ Characteristic Plant Shapes ❦

Here is a small selection of plants that illustrate differences in shape.

SHRUBLIKE PLANTS

Alpinia purpurata (red ginger)
Dracaena surculosa (gold-dust dracaena)
Monstera deliciosa (Swiss cheese plant)
Philodendron bipinnatifidum (fingerleaf philodendron)
Radermachera sinica (China doll plant)

TREELIKE PLANTS

Araucaria heterophylla (Norfolk Island pine)
Cordyline terminalis (ti plant)
Crassula ovata (jade plant)
Dracaena fragrans (decorator plant)
Ficus benjamina (weeping fig)
Ficus elastica 'Decora' (rubber tree)

FOUNTAIN-SHAPED PLANTS

Beaucarnea recurvata, aka *Nolina recurvata* (ponytail plant)
Cycas revoluta (sago palm)
Dieffenbachia amoena (dumbcane)
Guzmania lingulata (bromeliad)
Neoregelia spectabilis (fingernail plant)

CANOPYLIKE PLANTS

Polyscias fruticosa (ming tree, ming aralia)
Schefflera actinophylla (umbrella tree)
Schefflera elegantissima (false aralia)

ROSETTE-SHAPED PLANTS

Asplenium nidus (bird's nest fern)
Dracaena deremensis 'Warneckii'
Neoregelia carolinae (blushing bromeliad)

CASCADING PLANTS

Aeschynanthus speciosus (lipstick vine)
Asparagus densiflorus (emerald fern)
Begonia cultivars (angel-wing begonia)
Chlorophytum comosum (spider plant)
Epipremnum aureum (pothos)
Gynura aurantiaca (velvet plant)
Hedera helix (English ivy)
Nephrolepis exaltata 'Bostoniensis' (Boston fern)
Saxifraga stolonifera (strawberry geranium)
Setcreasea pallida (purple heart plant)
Syngonium podophyllum (arrowhead vine)
Zebrina pendula (wandering Jew)

One specimen plant, like this ficus, often is all that's needed to make a room feel more inviting. This plant's position near the window forms a connection with the greenery outside.

Leaf Size & Shape

The size and shape of a plant's leaves can determine to a large degree that plant's character. Individual leaves can range from tiny to quite large. Foliage can take many forms, from straight and sword-shaped to being divided into many small leaflets, like most fern fronds.

Smooth, pointed leaves can make a plant look majestic and elegant. Plants with this type of leaf are ti plant (*Cordyline terminalis*), yuccas, and dragon tree (*Dracaena concinna*). False aralia (*Schefflera elegantissima*) has an Oriental look, its serrated leaves resembling the delicate brush strokes of Japanese painting or calligraphy. The large agaves and *Trichocereus*, or *Echinopsis*, cacti are dramatic living sculptures. Swiss cheese plant (*Monstera deliciosa*) brings the jungle indoors, and Chinese fan palm (*Licuala grandis*) is formal.

A plant with large leaves can look bold and make a dramatic statement. For example, rubber tree (*Ficus elastica*) and fiddle-leaf fig (*F. lyrata*) need to be displayed in a large room. In a smaller room, a plant that has more slender leaves, such as butterfly palm (*Chrysalidocarpus lutescens*), with its airy, fountainlike fronds, is more appropriate.

Plants with scalloped leaves, such as some philodendrons, are often more decorative than plants with straight-edged leaves because scalloped leaves tend to look more graceful. Yet scalloped leaves

Sizes, shapes, and textures are carefully blended here, thereby creating a pleasing harmony of green.

The arching fronds of butterfly palm seem suited for the old-fashioned motif established by the antique rocking chair and the teddy bears.

can sometimes look too fussy. Small-leaved ming aralia (*Polyscias fruticosa*) looks quite frilly. Palms, which are so often associated with tropical designs, are more versatile, blending beautifully with both contemporary and traditional settings.

Leaf & Flower Color

In addition to foliage shape and size, consider foliage color. There are many shades and tones of green. For example, *Dracaena fragrans* has foliage that is almost apple green; the cultivar 'Massangeana', known as corn plant, has yellow stripes down the center of the leaves. Dark-leaved plants (look for varieties named 'Burgundy' or *purpurea*) tend to look heavy and massive, whereas plants that have light-colored leaves, such as arrowhead vine (*Syngonium*), look quite graceful and airy.

The gold and yellow tones in the foliage of these plants would add zest to any room. The flowering bromeliad (top right corner) has three distinct colors.

You can go a step further and choose flowering houseplants that coordinate with a room's color scheme. Look for plants with flowers that match, harmonize with, or contrast with the colors of carpets, drapes, and upholstery in a room. For example, in a room with a yellow color scheme, you might choose houseplants with flowers in harmonizing shades of gold and orange. Yet a spot of bright red could add a striking accent. If you'd prefer a lively, contrasting approach, choose blue and purple blooms for the yellow room. For a quieter, more unified look, choose flowers of a yellow shade that's close to the other yellows in the room, perhaps augmented with light green foliage. An elegant, formal room done in white and neutral wood tones would be enhanced by deep green foliage plants and perhaps blue or white flowers.

The deep green leaves of this ficus tree add warmth to this formal room. The tree also lends elegance to the table setting while making the space cozier.

This florist's collection of orchids allows you to select blooming plants without waiting for them to flower. Florists often sell blooming houseplants and gift plants.

Buying Plants

Houseplants can be purchased almost anywhere—florists, nurseries, garden centers, mail-order companies, home-improvement centers, and supermarkets. If you know what to look for and select carefully, you can buy healthy plants from each type of supplier.

RETAIL OUTLETS

Florists sell premium plants such as large philodendrons, ficus trees, cacti, and orchids in bloom. They also sell plants associated with the holidays, such as those described on page 20 in Chapter 1. Although plants from a florist tend to be more expensive than plants sold elsewhere, they will usually be of high quality, and reputable florists often will replace a specimen plant if something goes wrong with it. Besides, staff at florist shops tend to be quite knowledgeable and are usually able to recommend plants for your needs.

Nurseries, garden centers, and patio shops carry houseplants, and also stock outdoor plants, such as annuals, perennials, trees, and shrubs. These sources usually carry table and desk plants such as begonias, small bromeliads, a few palms, and some ferns at moderate to high prices. They also generally offer a good selection of hanging plants. Because these suppliers specialize in all kinds of plants, if you shop there ask to talk to someone on the staff who is particularly knowledgeable about houseplants.

Mail-order companies offer a good selection. They will ship even the largest plants. However, shipping costs are usually high. Also, you may need some acquaintance with scientific (botanical) names to be sure of ordering the exact plant you want. To help you in this regard, the Plant Profiles in Part II, beginning on page 108, list both scientific and common names.

Supermarkets, general merchandisers, and home-improvement centers often have a fairly large assortment of foliage and flowering plants, and sometimes staff there can offer good advice. If you know what to look for, you can get good

A wide assortment of houseplants, from flowering gems to foliage plants to hanging baskets, can be found at supermarkets, home-improvement centers, garden stores, and florists—and even through mail order.

A **specimen bird's nest fern** takes center stage in this showroom. Be sure to inspect plants closely for pests and diseases before you purchase them. To be safe, you can quarantine new plants for a few days and then reinspect them before placing them with your other plants.

buys and healthy plants. Most mega-stores receive new plants from their suppliers twice a week—Mondays and Thursdays. For the best selection, try to shop as soon as a new shipment has been stocked. Import stores sometimes have nurseries, but care and quality vary from store to store. Wherever you shop, consider that some plants sit so long in the store that they have cobwebs, and sometimes you'll even find plants infested with ants or other pests.

EXAMINE CLOSELY

Before you buy a plant, inspect it carefully. Plants that have been force-fed to grow quickly usually die quickly, too. Avoid plants with wan or limp leaves. You want perky, bright green foliage. Stems should be solid and firm, not limp. Be sure the plant looks fresh, not bruised or off color. Check with your finger to be sure that it is potted in soil and not a soilless mix that is mostly filler material. The pot should feel fairly heavy, not light as a feather, when you lift it.

It is vital that you inspect for insects and disease. Examine both tops and bottoms of leaves and the leaf axils (where leaves attach to stems). Brown or white streaks on leaves can indicate rot or plant disease. Chewed leaf edges mean that insects have been at work and might still be in the soil. Shake the plant gently; if whiteflies are present, the disturbed insects will fly around the plant like a cloud of tiny snowflakes. Never buy a plant if you see signs of insects or disease. Also, check the soil; avoid plants that are growing in dry, caked soil because they are usually drought stressed.

Examine plants carefully for signs of pests, disease or stress before you buy them. **Top photo**: The roots emerging from the bottom of the pot indicate that this plant should have been transplanted into a larger container; these roots have been exposed to the air and have probably dried out. **Above**: The white stains are signs of fertilizer salt buildup. This plant may be stressed; look for another. **Right**: Do not buy a plant with limp or yellow leaves. The leggy growth with long stems and few leaves is another sign of trouble.

Large potted plants transform this functional space into an inviting transitional area. Here, large jars and the sand-colored tile floor convey a Southwestern feel.

Indoor Conditions

Successfully matching plants to room conditions can mean the difference between a healthy plant and one that must be discarded after a short time. Conditions in the average home or apartment vary from room to room and from daytime to nighttime. Temperature, light, and humidity are key factors. Consider the various room environments in your home, and try to determine which plants will work best in each.

HALLS AND ENTRYWAYS

People form their first impression of your home inside the entry, but in many homes this is hardly a hospitable place for plants. If the space is large enough, a plant on a pedestal can lend an elegant look. If there is a reception table, use a small plant such as prayer plant (*Maranta*) or a small bromeliad such as *Cryptanthus*.

If the hall is barren, think about using a single large plant in place of a piece of furniture. Cascading plants placed on tables or shelves in halls will soften the sharp lines of furniture and

hardware. Always use appropriate mats, saucers, or other protective devices so that water leaking from drainage holes does not damage furnishings.

Drafts and Light. The hall or entry may have temperatures of 65° to 75°F. But doors opening and closing allow cold drafts that cause problems for some plants. In winter, an open door can give plants an arctic blast, which can kill or severely damage any but the toughest plants. Often, halls and entryways have little natural light. In this case, choose plants that tolerate low light levels. Yet even these plants may need more light.

To give plants more light, you can install ceiling lights aimed at the plants or move the plants to brighter locations periodically to help them regain their strength. You can also put the plants outside in summer to replenish their vigor. The box on the next page lists some plants that will survive the ins and outs of halls and entryways.

The plants give this dramatic stairway a more appealing, less formidable scale. They also break up the plain expanse of hallway behind the stairs.

A single arching palm can work wonders for an otherwise sparsely furnished living room. This palm fills the gap between the two sofas, echoes the green in the large painting, and—not least brings nature indoors.

LIVING ROOMS AND DINING ROOMS

These generally large rooms tend to be bright, with natural light and usually have even, moderate temperatures of 65° to 75°F. These conditions make most living rooms good places for plants. Plants can contribute to living rooms and dining rooms in a number of ways. Large plants, thoughtfully placed, can lend a sense of organization to the space and direct the flow of traffic. Small plants can accent the decor and provide their own interest. Study the light levels in different parts of your living room or dining room to see where plants could thrive. Then think about the plant forms that would complement the architecture, space, and furnishings. With all this in mind, you can begin selecting plants. (See "Shape & Growth Habit," pages 36–37, for information on plant forms.)

Large plants are generally well suited to spacious living rooms and dining rooms because the plants don't look out of scale there. If the room is long and narrow, choose an upright plant with slender branches, such as a specimen dragon tree (*Dracaena concinna*). If the architecture is modern and the decor contemporary, consider a large, sculptural cactus. Such plants are especially striking in modern interiors.

This dining area needs the low planter near the expanse of windows as much as the flowering plants themselves need to be positioned near the light. The attractive planter does not obscure the view.

When plant colors contrast with walls, they help make large rooms more intimate. The plants at the far end of the room add a bright highlight to muted walls and furnishings.

Tight Space. If your floor space is limited, consider hanging baskets of ferns or tropical trailers from the ceiling. For greater impact, try positioning the baskets at three different heights. To break the monotony of walls that are mainly windows, use medium-size plants, perhaps in groups of three, to bring color and life to the blank area. Such plants will benefit from the excellent light.

Plants as Accents. If you have a fireplace, you could set a few plants on the hearth to draw attention to this feature of the room. However, because of the heat and dryness created when a fire is burning, it's essential to remove the plants then. Another likely place for plants in living rooms and dining rooms is behind a table and chairs, to supply vertical accents. Instead of placing a long table behind a sofa, try a row of identical plants in identically colored containers. Install lighting fixtures to ensure that the plants receive sufficient light.

Once the large plants are in place, add a few complementary table or desk plants to pull the room together. The goal is to balance the large plants with smaller plants placed around the room, not to make your living room look like a plant shop. You can move the small plants around from time to time to change the look of the room.

Color Considerations. When plant color contrasts with wall color, the plant draws the eye, often making a large room feel smaller and more intimate. Consider the drama created by a cascading, brightly colored gesneriad such as *Episcia* 'Flame' against an off-white wall. If there is no nearby window light, install a spotlight or track lighting. (See "Light," pages 58–63, for more information on artificial light.)

Conversely, for a small living room, select plants with leaves similar in value and color to the walls; plants that echo room colors make a room seem larger. Another way to create the illusion of greater space is to group plants toward the center of the room. Avoid blocking the traffic flow.

If you have limited floor space, look up. Here, a trailing plant is displayed beautifully atop a corner curio cabinet.

BEDROOMS

There was a time when people didn't keep plants in their bedrooms because they believed the plants would deplete oxygen levels and make breathing difficult. Actually, the opposite is true—plants give off oxygen during the day as a byproduct of photosynthesis. Plants also improve air quality by absorbing pollutants, while creating a relaxing ambiance. Graceful palms or ferns on bed tables or in hanging containers are especially fitting.

Contemporary bedrooms are often designed for both living and sleeping. In a bedroom divided into sleeping, dressing, and sitting areas, you can use plants in imaginative yet functional ways to create the feeling of an indoor garden. For example, you can place about three tall plants in a row to create a divider or natural screen between the different parts of the room. Keep a watering can in a nearby bathroom so that you can water the plants easily.

Plants in bedrooms improve the air quality while creating a tranquil atmosphere. **Above**: The fern and the palm in the bedroom lend a sheltered, cozy feel to this space. **Left**: The ficus tree in this more traditional bedroom adds needed color and visually raises the wall height.

BATHROOMS

Today's newer homes generally have large bathrooms. These luxurious rooms—often a cross between a spa and a traditional bathroom—need plants to soften the hard look of tile, chrome, glass, and marble, and to make the space friendlier.

Bathrooms can be excellent locations for plants. In fact, many plants grow better in bathrooms than in any other place in a home. The warm, humid conditions there help make tropical plants grow well. Also, many bathrooms have frosted or patterned glass windowpanes, which provide diffused light that is neither too bright nor too dim—exactly what most plants prefer.

Decorating Ideas. Floor plants are ideal for a large bathroom, and there is usually ample space for them. Smaller plants, such as orchids and bromeliads, can suggest the tropics. Vanities and tables offer innumerable places on which plants can be displayed.

If your bathroom is small, consider placing a hanging fern or other basket plant near the window or installing glass shelves across the

The warm, humid conditions of bathrooms help tropical plants thrive. The plants shown here soften the hard edges of the tile and help transform this oversize bathroom into a spa.

window to create platforms for small plants. Another option is to place a vertical plant stand or plant pole in a bright corner to accommodate several smaller plants on different levels. In a bathroom without windows, plants can thrive if placed close to fluorescent lights that are kept on 12 to 16 hours a day.

Even though tropical plants are particularly well suited to both the environment and style of many bathrooms, you should be bold in trying all kinds of plants there, including those that aren't doing well elsewhere. Plants really perk up in the brighter light and higher humidity of the bathroom. The only plants to avoid placing in bathrooms are those that prefer drier conditions, and many of the plants with fuzzy or hairy leaves.

Well-selected plants can thrive under bathroom skylights. And the daily higher doses of humidity in the bathroom can complement good lighting to provide excellent growing conditions.

KITCHENS

Modern kitchens tend to be large, natural centers of activity often located near a recreation or morning room. There is usually plenty of bright light from windows or skylights and ample humidity from cooking, so plants can do well in kitchens. There, your favorite plants can lend a personal touch and extend a cheerful, colorful welcome to all who gather.

Shelves, cabinet tops, and windowsills are all prime places for small potted plants. Flowering plants such as African violets, geraniums, and miniature begonias grow luxuriantly in bright, humid kitchens. Dozens of medium-size foliage plants, such as prayer plants (*Maranta*), arrow-head vines (*Syngonium*), and peperomias, also do well. In a large kitchen where you want a green look, consider a floor plant such as a large lady palm (*Rhapis*) or sago palm (*Cycas*).

White and yellow are two favorite color schemes for kitchens. In a white or yellow room, plants with apple green or variegated foliage look splendid. For a unified look, put all the plants in pots of the same color.

Kitchens become more inviting when decorated with plants. In the two kitchen photos here, the dead space above cabinets is put to good use with plant displays. **Above**: The upper tier of plants benefits from skylighting, and the flowering plants benefit from artificial light. **Left**: The ficus tree enjoys window light, while anchoring the dining area. **Below**: Pots of the same color help unify the display.

If you're looking for compact plants to grow on a sunny kitchen windowsill or under lights, consider culinary herbs. Their flavor will be milder than that of herbs grown outdoors, and their leaves will be smaller, but you can still use them to perk up midwinter recipes.

Recommended indoor herbs include basil, chives, bay, mints, marjoram, oregano, rosemary, and parsley. You'll need several pots of the herbs you use most.

The best indoor location for herbs is a warm, sunny south- or west-facing window that receives a minimum of six hours of sun a day. Turn the pots every day or two so the stems grow reasonably straight. If you grow herbs under fluorescent lights, keep the lamps 5 to 6 inches above the tops of the plants, and leave them on for 14 hours a day. (For more on artificial lighting, see pages 60–61.)

Plant herbs in 6-inch pots with a porous, all-purpose potting mix that is equal parts potting soil, sand, and peat moss. Start new plants from seeds or cuttings, as explained in Chapter 6.

Fertilize the herbs monthly with an all-purpose liquid fertilizer. Avoid overfertilizing, or your herbs

An abundance of herbs thrives in this sunny window. Herbs need at least six hours of light a day.

will grow too quickly and have poor flavor. Herbs don't like soggy soil. So let the soil dry slightly between waterings, and then water when the soil feels dry just below the surface.

Most herbs thrive in temperatures of 65° to 68°F indoors, with a slight dip at night. Plenty of humidity and good air circulation are also important. If your herbs are on a windowsill, move them back from the glass during very cold winter weather.

To use herbs in cooking, wait to cut their leaves until the moment they are needed.

Leafy culinary herbs (above) in matching hand-painted pots please both the eye and the palate. **Left**: Herbs grown in the kitchen provide the indoor gardener with satisfying plant work and the cook with wonderful flavor enhancers.

Bay Leaf

Rosemary

Basil

Spearmint

Oregano

Parsley

Chives

Marjoram

chapter
FOUR

Houseplant Containers

*T*his chapter describes some of the most functional, attractive, and widely used types of houseplant containers.

Virtually any vessel that can hold soil and allows drainage can be used as a plant container. Baskets, tubs, terra-cotta pots, decorated pots, glazed ceramic jardinieres, Victorian-style urns, wine casks, boxes, terrariums—the list goes on. You can also use decorative containers, called *cachepots*, without drainage holes, to hold smaller planted pots with drainage holes. As long as containers allow good drainage and are the appropriate size, they will work well for your houseplants.

When selecting a houseplant container, be sure to consider its appearance, its proportion in relation to plant size, and the material of which it is made.

Terra-cotta pot with a raised relief design is a classic choice. Terra-cotta (literally *earth-fired*) complements almost any plant color or decorating style.

Hanging Containers

Hanging pots and baskets come in many sizes and are made of various materials. There are slotted redwood baskets, in which you place a potted plant; woven baskets lined with plastic; plastic pots with hangers attached; and wire baskets meant to be lined with peat moss or sphagnum.

Hanging containers hold plants that add beauty and color at eye level. This Congo fig combines a trailing habit with upright growth—an interesting choice to hang.

There are also ceramic hanging pots—some decorated, some plain—with attached saucers. In addition, there are simple, attractive wrought-iron hanging containers. Whichever type you choose, be sure the container has the means of catching excess water that will drain from the soil.

HANGING HARDWARE

You also need some means of suspending a container from a ceiling or a wall. Chains are usually the most attractive answer; they come in different sizes and colors. Or you can use sturdy wire or clear monofilament fishing line. For an informal look, try woven and macramé hangers to convert conventional pots into hanging containers.

No matter what kind of hanger you use, be sure it can support the weight of the plant and pot. An 8-inch diameter container filled with damp soil can weigh approximately 50 pounds.

For ceiling attachments, all you need is a screw hook. When you install the hook, embed it into a ceiling joist or a structurally strong surface, such as wood, so that the screw threads have a firm hold. Even with lightweight plants, it's unwise to depend on the structural integrity of gypsum or acoustic ceiling panels themselves. (See the options for securing hanging pots on pages 56–57.)

Although you can grow almost any plant in a hanging container, cascading or trailing plants look better in hanging motifs than upright plants.

PLANTS FOR HANGING CONTAINERS
Acalypha hispida (chenille plant)
Aeschynanthus (lipstick plant)
Begonia, angel-wing types
Chlorophytum comosum (spider plant)
Columnea (columnea)
Epipremnum aureum (pothos)
Episcia (flame violet)
Ferns
Hoya (wax plant)
Nematanthus (goldfish plant)
Philodendron (philodendron)
Sedum morganianum (burro's tail)
Zebrina (wandering Jew)

Hanging in a window, this flowering lipstick plant eliminates the need for any other window treatments.

A hanging basket filled with variegated ivy trails over small plants peeking out from below.

Pots

Pots can be made of unglazed terra-cotta, glazed pottery, or various kinds of plastic.

TERRA-COTTA POTS

Simple terra-cotta pots are available in diameters of 3 to 24 inches and in a range of depths. These pots are inexpensive, and their earth tones complement practically all plant colors. *Note:* Soil dries out quickly in terra-cotta pots because their walls are porous. But this can be a plus because it prevents plants from becoming waterlogged. Soak all types of terra-cotta pots overnight before planting in them. Otherwise the containers will absorb moisture that the plants need from the soil. You can find terra-cotta pots at nurseries and garden centers, in the plant section of general merchandisers, in supermarkets, and at many florists.

Variations of the classic terra-cotta pot include cylindrical containers, strawberry jars (which have small planting pockets on the sides), pots shaped like animals and birds, and shallow azalea or fern pots. The basic cylindrical pot is available in three sizes, with a maximum 14-inch diameter.

The azalea pot is squatty, three-quarters as high as it is wide, and 6 to 14 inches in diameter. It

Pots and plants of various sizes and shapes sometimes look best if the pots are of a uniform color. Here, the terra-cotta color helps showcase the whole composition.

These containers include a plastic planter box (top left), simulated concrete (top right), an orchid pot with slots (lower right) and a shallow bulb pot (far left).

This three-legged urn is an elegant container for *Paphiopedilum* orchids. The simplicity of the container suits the plant well.

Glazed ceramic container compliments narcissus and pansies. Colors, shape, and scale combine to make this arrangement perfection-in-a-pot.

Glazed decorative pots set off these colored flowers without competing with the blooms. To avoid water damage on furniture, it's best to water plants on a separate trolley or at the sink.

often looks to be in better proportion to plants than the typical narrow clay pot.

Italian terra-cotta pots can have rims of varied shapes— a tight lip, a round edge, a beveled edge, or a wavy edge. All these variations can be attractive. Venetian pots are barrel-shaped, with a band design pressed into the sides. These formal-looking containers are sold in 8- to 20-inch sizes. The graceful Spanish pots have outward sloping sides and flared lips. Their walls are heavier than those of conventional clay pots, and diameters range from 8 to 12 inches.

Three-legged pots are bowl-shaped and raise plants up, putting them on better display. They are 8 to 20 inches in diameter. Bulb pans or seed bowls generally are less than half as high as they are wide. These containers look rather like deep saucers; they are sold in 6- to 12-inch sizes.

GLAZED POTS

Glazed pots are usually used to impart a more formal and elegant look to plant displays. But you cannot plant directly in most glazed pots because they have no drainage holes. To use your favorite glazed pot, put a plain plastic or unglazed terra-cotta pot with a drainage hole inside the decorative container.

PLASTIC POTS

Plastic pots are lightweight and easy to clean. Because plastic is not porous, be careful not to overwater; waterlogging the plant can cause root rot. Also, because of their light weight, plastic pots may become unstable and tip over when planted with heavy specimen plants.

This shallow glazed pot houses a colorful cymbidium. Here the low pot perfectly suits the plants, though it conceals an inner pot with necessary drainage holes.

Cachepots are made of various materials. They are usually used to hold planted pots set on a layer of pebbles or shard to aid drainage.

CACHEPOTS

These decorative containers usually hold plain pots with drainage holes. Place the planted pots atop a layer of pebbles or gravel into which excess water can drain. Porcelain cachepots may be splashed with flower or fruit designs, often with gold accents. Brass or copper cachepots are rich looking and not overly expensive. Mahogany and teak cachepots provide a unique look but are expensive. Some cachepots are hexagonal-shaped, with footed bases.

Tubs and Urns

Tubs can be round or hexagonal and made of wood, stone, or concrete. The best wooden tubs are durable, rot-resistant redwood or cypress. Stone or concrete tubs can look good indoors in a sunroom. Japanese soy tubs are inexpensive and appropriate for informal family rooms and dens. They are widely available. Blue-glazed Japanese porcelain tubs are formal and rich-looking, especially when they contain small, treelike plants such as jade plants (*Crassula ovata*).

Urns come in a variety of shapes and sizes and usually have a pedestal or footed base attached. They may be made of fiberglass to simulate stone,

A shallow terra-cotta pot is ideal for this dish garden of succulents and cacti.

bronze, concrete, or other materials. Urns look best when viewed at eye level, such as at the end of a sunroom shelf. Flowering houseplants look especially attractive in urns. Although pedestal urns are handsome, their large size can make them appear overpowering in a small room, so reserve their use for large, grand spaces.

Boxes

Small indoor trees and shrubs look especially good in simple wooden boxes. The wood complements the stems and trunks of the plants, and the solid structure of the box provides a visual base for the plants. A layer of moist unmilled peat, or sphagnum, moss on top of the soil lends an airy touch to the container, keeping it from looking too heavy. Because a wooden box filled with soil and plants can be quite heavy, keep wheeled trolleys (sometimes called dollies) under these containers so you move them easily. (See "Pedestals, Stands, Trolleys," on the next page.)

Choosing Containers

Select a container that complements the plant's appearance and growth habit. Bushy, round plants are often complemented by bowl-or

A glazed cachepot planted with a bromeliad makes a lovely centerpiece on the table. The pot is just tall enough to hide the base of the plant.

dish-shaped pots. Tall vertical plants often look best in cylindrical containers.

Also consider pot depth. Some plants have shallow roots; others have long roots. A plant with an extensive root system needs a deep container, while a plant with few roots, such as a bromeliad, needs only a shallow pot. The pot should comfortably accommodate the plant's roots but should not be so big that the plant looks lost in it. Besides, too much "unused" soil tends to get soggy and rot the roots.

Container color is another important consideration. When in doubt, opt for understated colors. Bold colors clash with most home surroundings, while white or dark green are generally complementary to furnishings. Terracotta blends beautifully with most interiors.

A simple glazed pot is an effective container for this casual collection of plants.

When growing potted plants on windowsills, tabletops, or other furniture, protect the surfaces from water stains. Buy plastic or terra-cotta saucers to match the pots. Saucers are available in diameters from 4 inches to 28 inches. Many terra-cotta saucers are unglazed, so moisture still seeps through if it is left in the saucer. Look for saucers with glazed bottoms, or put a cork mat or felt protector under the saucer. This is certainly important when you place plants on fine furniture.

Pedestals, Stands, Trolleys

You can buy an array of plant stands, pedestals, and other decorative display furniture to show off your plants. Most stands are made of wood, wrought iron, or plastic and raise plants nearer eye level. Besides making plants look attractive, a grate-like stand or platform can help air reach plant roots. Elevated stands, actually pedestals, vary in height from 12 to 60 inches and generally support a single plant. There are also wrought-iron stands designed to display six or eight pots and fitted with iron rings to hold plants in place.

Plant trolleys (sometimes called "dollies") are wooden platforms with wheels or large plastic saucers with wheels. These movable "stages" offer a good means of moving big plants around. (*Note:* You need to move plants to the sink or put a saucer underneath them when it's time to water.) The units also raise plants off the floor and thus help prevent water from staining wood surfaces.

The wooden plant stand, top left, elevates plants to table level. The plastic saucer on wheels is one type of plant dollie that is used to move plants around. The waffle grill and round disks protect furniture from moisture damage.

How to Install Supports for Hanging Plants

Although it's important to position hanging plants where they will be most attractive, it's more important that they be securely hung. These pages show how to find structural support and install hardware. *Note*: Rot-weakened wood won't be a reliable support, and some plants greatly increase in weight as they grow.

Installing Bridging

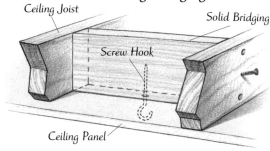

If ceiling joists are not directly above the point where you wish to suspend a plant and you have access to joists from above, you can create solid wood bridging before driving the screw hook.

Attaching Hooks to Ceiling Joists

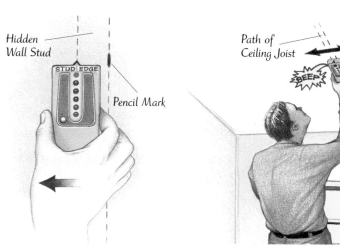

1 A battery-powered stud finder detects differing densities behind surfaces. It lights up and beeps when it detects the leading edge of a stud and shuts off when it passes the stud.

2 To locate ceiling joists or wall studs, slide the stud finder perpendicular to likely supports, and lightly mark exact edges. This lets you drill holes into exact centers of supports for maximum holding power.

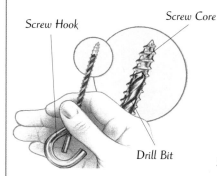

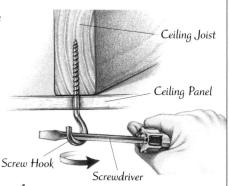

3 Before drilling a pilot hole for the screw, visually compare the diameter of the screw shaft with that of the drill bit. The bit diameter should be no greater than that of the solid core of the screw.

4 After starting the screw hook by hand, turn the hook portion by means of a screwdriver or pliers. Drive the screw hook deep enough so that all threads bite into solid wood.

Attaching a Base Plate

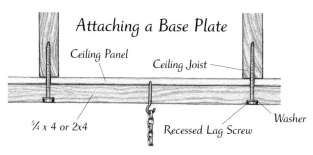

If you don't have access to the joists from above, you can create a solid base for screw hooks in various positions by attaching a thick wooden plate to two or more ceiling joists. Fasten the base plate to the joist by means of recessed lag screws and washers.

Installing a Hanging Pole

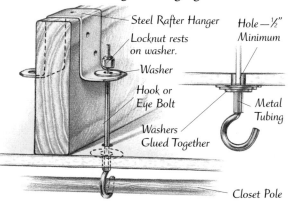

If you have access to the joists from above, you can suspend a closet pole perpendicular to ceiling joists with steel hangers and hook or eye bolts. This assembly allows sturdy support, and it lets you slide plants along the pole.

Decorative Ceiling Hooks

Decorative ceiling hooks sometimes come in packets with an optional screw and toggle bolt. *Caution*: Packaging on smaller hooks (screw threads a mere ¾ inch long) may suggest that the hooks can support up to 30 pounds, but this assumes ideal installations.

Installing a Decorative Hook.
A toggle bolt has more holding power in gypsum ceiling panels than a mere screw, but its effectiveness depends on the support of weak panels, which could become even weaker if damp. If you employ this light-duty assembly, follow manufacturer's installation instructions, but use plants weighing no more than 5 pounds (no heavier than a half gallon of milk). Installation steps:

1 Drill a hole just large enough for the folded wings of the spring-loaded toggle, usually ⅝ inch or larger.
2 Insert the assembled toggle bolt.
3 Pull gently downward on the spring-activated wings so that they bite into paneling as you turn the hook to drive the threaded portion of the bolt upward.
4 Stop when the wings and plate are snug.

Decorative Hook

Small Hook with Screw. Never drive a decorative screw hook into unsupported drywall (gypsum) panels. Such an installation allows only a few turns of the screw thread to bite into flimsy support material. See proper installation below.

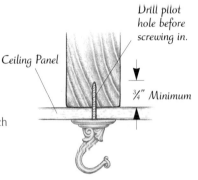

Drill pilot hole before screwing in.

Ceiling Panel

¾" Minimum

Instead of driving this screw hook into unsupported ceiling paneling, drive the screw through the panel into a ceiling joist so nearly all screw threads bite into wood. (See "Attaching Hooks to Ceiling Joists" on previous page. When selecting a drill bit, follow the manufacturer's recommendations or use the technique illustrated in Step 3 on the previous page.)

Spring-Loaded Wings

Decorative Plate

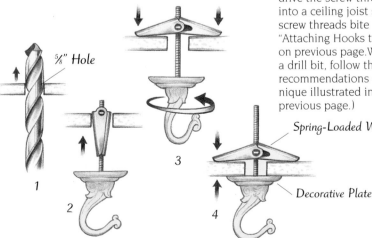

⅝" Hole

1

2

3

4

Wall Brackets

Wall brackets for lightweight plants come in assorted shapes and sizes. Most screw-mount into wall studs. For guidance on finding wall studs, follow instructions on the previous page. Packaging usually includes screws of suitable length for the bracket size and plant-carrying capacity.

Swinging-Arm Brackets

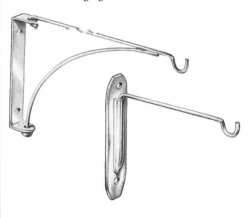

Fixed-Arm Brackets

chapter
FIVE

Raising & Grooming

*I*t takes more than sufficient light and good potting soil to grow healthy plants. Other cultural needs, such as fertilizer, water, temperature, humidity, and air circulation, must also be met. Each of these factors in a plant's environment interacts with and is affected by the others. Although you don't need to provide perfect conditions for a plant to thrive, you must provide a reasonably appropriate balance among the various factors so that plants will prosper and reward your efforts with beautiful foliage and flowers. This chapter explains good growing conditions and how to optimize them.

Houseplants outgrow their pots, making repotting part of their care. Generally, plants this size and smaller should be put into pots one size larger, every year— larger plants, every two years.

Light

Without light, plants will die. Light is necessary for *photosynthesis*, the production of sugar and starches from carbon dioxide and water. How long a plant is exposed to light each day—the *daylength*, or *photoperiod*—determines the amount of food the plant manufactures and whether the plant grows well and produces flowers.

DAYLENGTHS

Some plants, called *short-day plants*, will not bloom unless they receive enough hours of darkness each day. Christmas cactus, which flowers in winter, is a good example of a short-day plant. *Long-day plants*, on the other hand, need long days to set buds. Summer bloomers, such as most of the familiar garden annuals and orchids, are long-day plants.

Other plants, such as African violets, are considered *day-neutral*, which means they are not particular about daylength and will flower at various times of the year. If you want to grow flowering houseplants under artificial light, you can use their daylength needs to determine how many hours a day to keep lights on for them. See the box, "Daylength Needs of Plants," on the next page for guidance on special light needs of some of the plants profiled in Part II of this book.

58
RAISING & GROOMING

Window light requirements vary from plant to plant. **Above**: Cool, indirect light from a north window is perfect for the fern and the Chinese evergreen. **Right**: The strong heat and light of a south-facing window are well suited to this cactus container garden.

WINDOW LIGHT

The amount and intensity of light entering your windows depends on the exposure and whether the light is obstructed.

Southern. A south-facing window is brightest, and plants on south windowsills may receive direct sun for much of the day. South light is too intense for many plants, and some will sunburn—you may notice a darkening or "burning" of their leaves. South windows are also hot, so be sure not to let plants growing in these windows dry out.

To soften the light from a south window, place a sheer curtain between the pane and the plants. Good plants for south windows include cacti and succulents, amaryllis, geraniums, and many other plants grown mainly for their flowers.

Eastern and Western. East windows are the next brightest and an ideal location for many plants. An east window gets cool, bright morning sun and indirect light in the afternoon.

West windows are reasonably bright but can become quite warm when lit by the hot afternoon sun. The best plants for west windows are those that can tolerate heat.

Northern. A north window receives indirect light all day, and is the coolest, dimmest exposure. Not many flowering plants will thrive in a north window without supplemental light, but plenty of foliage plants will do well.

Flowering plants and those with variegated leaves need the brightest light, while foliage plants and ferns need the least. Many houseplants are native to jungles and rain forests, where the light is filtered through the trees. For these plants, sunny southern windows can be fatal.

Intensity. From all exposures, light levels decrease dramatically the farther away from the window you go. In the center of a room, light may be only half as intense as the light on a windowsill. You can increase light for plants if you have reflective surfaces nearby.

TOO MUCH OR TOO LITTLE LIGHT

Most houseplants thrive where they receive bright or dappled light from a window, without direct sun. Learn to observe your plants for signs that they're getting too much or not enough light.

Plants that aren't receiving enough light respond by "reaching" toward the light source. Their stems grow long and spindly and often curve in the direction of the nearest window. Also, their leaves will be fewer and smaller than normal and spaced farther apart on the stems.

Plants receiving too much light often turn pale green and eventually yellowish, a symptom that can be mistaken for lack of nutrients. The leaves may curl downward, which might look like symptoms of underwatering.

If you see such symptoms in your plants, consider all the elements of their environment—including light—before attempting to adjust the conditions.

Artificial Light

Plants evolved in nature in response to the sun's spectrum of wavelengths, so artificial lighting tends to increase in effectiveness the more it emulates natural light. Try to choose plants that will do well in the natural light of your home, and then supplement with artificial light as needed.

The important factors are the duration and intensity of the light, and the spectrum wavelengths present. Plants need the blue, red, and far-red wavelengths of the spectrum to grow normally. Blue enables plants to manufacture carbohydrates. Red controls assimilation and affects a plant's response to the relative length

Artificial lights, used in a combination of spectrums, enable houseplants to thrive in the absence of sufficient natural light.

of light and darkness. And far-red controls seed germination, stem length, and leaf size.

If the duration and light levels in your rooms are insufficient, you will probably need to provide supplemental light. This is especially important if your windows face north or if tall buildings or trees block light for part of the day.

INCANDESCENT LIGHT

Incandescent light bulbs can help plants grow somewhat, but they emit only the red-orange part of the spectrum and thus aren't sufficient on their own. And about 70 percent of their energy is wasted as heat. As an alternative, incandescent floodlights have built-in reflectors that concentrate light more efficiently. Yet like standard bulbs, they provide only the red wavelengths. And if placed too close to plants, their heat will dry out both the plants and their soil.

As supplemental light, incandescents can be useful during the shorter days of winter. In this case, a 200-watt floodlight placed 2 to 3 feet from a foliage plant supplies needed light without overheating and drying the plant.

FLUORESCENT LIGHT

Fluorescent lights are more popular for house-plants than incandescents for many reasons. First, they burn cooler and can be placed much closer to plants. Also, they give more light (lumens) per watt than incandescents. Fluorescents are available in an array of sizes and configurations, and as special grow lamps that resemble incandescent floodlights. In addition, fluorescent lights are available in various wattages, as well as in various wavelengths that allow you to use them in combination or singly to approximate sunlight.

Types of Fluorescents. For houseplants, there are three main types of fluorescents to consider:

✣ Cool-white tubes, which have enhanced blues

✣ Warm-white tubes, which have enhanced reds

✣ Special growing lamps, which emit a broad range of wavelengths, including blue, red, and far-red. (These may be advertised as wide-spectrum or full-spectrum lamps and provide more red and blue than standard fluorescents do. They screw into regular sockets, but they emit unnatural-looking light.)

Combining Lights. For a pleasing look, you can combine cool-white fluorescents with warm-whites. Or you can combine cool-white fluorescents with incandescents, thereby providing a relatively full spectrum and good looks. But position the incandescents farther from the plants.

The necessary distance between fluorescent lights and plants varies with the type of plant

LIGHTING RULE OF THUMB

If your room lacks sufficient natural light, keep artificial lights on for 12 to 14 hours a day for foliage plants and 16 to 18 hours for flowering plants. Automatic timers are handy for ensuring that plants are getting enough light (for the right amount of time.)

and its stage of growth. Some plants need to be 3 inches from the lights; others, 12 to 15 inches.

Give germinating seeds and cuttings 10 lamp watts per square foot of growing area. Most foliage plants need 15 watts per square foot. High-energy flowering plants need 20 watts per square foot. If you supplement fluorescents with incandescents to get the vital far-red wavelengths, use a 4:1 ratio. Thus, if you are providing 200 watts of fluorescent light, add 50 watts of incandescent light. Temper these guidelines with common sense. Move plants farther from the lights if the leaves look burned or if colors fade. Move plants closer if growth is spindly.

Note: Because fluorescent lamps gradually lose their effectiveness over time, it's wise to replace them annually even if they look okay.

METAL HALIDE & MERCURY-VAPOR LIGHTS

These high-intensity, expensive lamps provide relatively full-spectrum light but tend to be used more by professional growers. Be sure to follow the manufacturer's suggestions for their placement.

The ceiling incandescent lamp (above) is an attractive means of displaying and providing growing light for this lush fern. **Right**: This full-spectrum mercury-vapor floodlight delivers a balance of the blue-red and far-red wavelengths.

How to Build a Knockdown Growing Stand

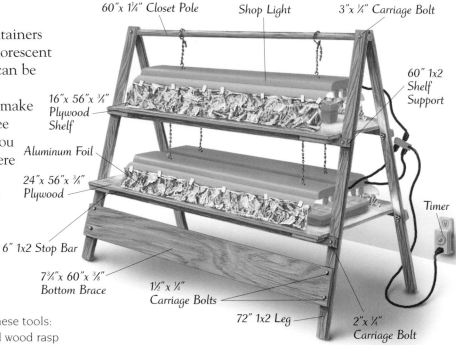

This stand supports an array of containers for raising seedlings under three fluorescent shop lights. For storage, the stand can be quickly disassembled.

You don't have to own a saw to make this stand. A home-center employee can cut the plywood for you, and you can probably borrow a handsaw there to cut the 1x2 lumber and closet pole. The cut wood fits into a mid-size car for transport.

Designed by Rita Buchanan
Illustrated by Steve Buchanan

Photo labels:
60"x 1¼" Closet Pole
Shop Light
3"x ¼" Carriage Bolt
60" 1x2 Shelf Support
16"x 56"x ⅜" Plywood Shelf
Aluminum Foil
24"x 56"x ⅜" Plywood
Timer
6" 1x2 Stop Bar
7¾"x 60"x ⅜" Bottom Brace
1½" x ¼" Carriage Bolts
72" 1x2 Leg
2"x ¼" Carriage Bolt

Tools
With wood precut, you'll need these tools:
- Screwdriver, framing square, and wood rasp
- Drill with ⅜-, ¼-, and ⁷⁄₆₄-inch bits, and one smaller bit for the screw hooks you select

Materials
Lumber: As shown below and right
Lights: Three 48-inch fluorescent shop lights with hanging chains
Fasteners: As shown in photo below

2	3" x ¼" carriage bolts
8	2" x ¼" carriage bolts
4	1½" x ¼" carriage bolts
16	¼" wingnuts
4	1" screw hooks or cuphooks
16	#6 x 1" flathead screws

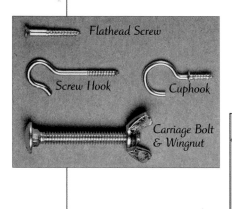

Flathead Screw
Screw Hook
Cuphook
Carriage Bolt & Wingnut

⅜" Plywood Cutting Diagram

16"
24"
Approx. 7¾"
Top Shelf
Bottom Shelf
Bottom Brace
56"
60"

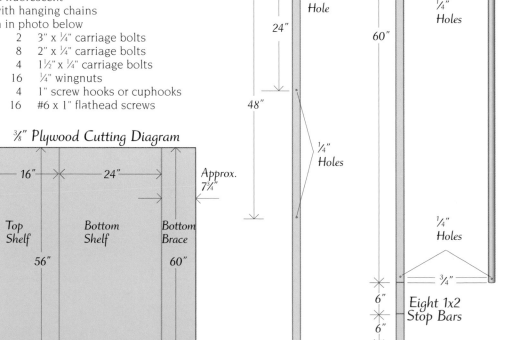

Four 72" 1x2 Legs
1"
⅜" Hole
24"
48"
¼" Holes

Four 60" 1x2 Shelf Supports
60"
6"

One 60"x 1¼" Closet Pole
¾"
¼" Holes
¼" Holes
¾"

Eight 1x2 Stop Bars
6"
6"

Growing Seedlings under Shop Lights

CUTTING AND ASSEMBLY

(All wood dimensions are shown on the previous page.)

1 Cut a ⅜-inch sheet of plywood for the two shelves and the bottom brace.

2 Use four 6-foot lengths of 1x2 lumber for the legs.

3 From four other 6-foot 1x2s, first cut the four 60-inch shelf supports and then the eight 6-inch stop bars.

4 Cut a 60x1¼-inch closet pole, and drill ¼-inch holes ¾ inch from each end.

LEGWORK

5 Drill ⅜-inch holes 1 inch from the top of each leg.

6 Mark and drill two ¼-inch holes in each of the four legs and shelf supports as shown on the previous page.

7 Using a wood rasp, make a shallow indentation near the top of each leg to accommodate the closet pole. (See below.) Note: Extend the indentation farther above the hole (toward the top of the leg); after assembly, this allows the legs to swing open without binding.

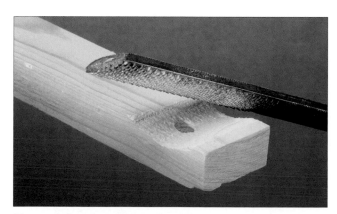

Shaping Indentations Using a Wood Rasp

8 Place two legs on the floor, parallel and about 60 inches apart with the rasped indentation down, and place the bottom brace on the legs about 10 inches from the leg bottoms. Use a framing square, as shown at right, to align one end of the brace with that leg. Then, with scrap wood underneath the leg, drill two ¼-inch holes through both the brace and the leg. Repeat at the other end of the brace. Then insert four 1½x¼-inch carriage bolts through the holes, and tighten the wingnuts to fasten the brace to the leg.

¼" Holes

Framing Square

Squaring the Bottom Brace

9 Lean the leg and brace assembly against a wall, and fasten the two shelf supports by means of 2x¼-inch carriage bolts and wingnuts.

10 As in the preceding step, lean the remaining two legs against a wall, and fasten their two shelf supports.

11 As shown at right, sandwich the closet pole between the rasped indentations at the top ends of mating legs, and fasten with a 3x¼-inch carriage bolt and wingnut.

SHELVES

12 Position stop bars under the corners of each shelf, flush with the shelf edge. Drill a ⁷⁄₆₄-inch hole through the first stop bar into the shelf, and fasten with a #6 x 1-inch flathead screw. Drill and fasten a second screw before repeating the process at each corner.

Sandwiching the Closet Pole

PUTTING IT ALL TOGETHER

13 Using a drill bit no larger in diameter than the solid core of your screw hooks or cuphooks, drill and then screw the hooks into the bottom of the top shelf supports, about 10 inches from the ends.

14 After spreading the legs approximately as shown in the drawing, place the shelves on their supports. Hang the bottom shop lights, and tie the top one in place.

15 For waterproofing, apply exterior paint or wood sealer.

Soil

Unlike most garden plants, houseplants are in containers and cannot send their roots far down through the soil to seek water and nutrients. So it is up to you to supply the right balance of nutrients and moisture. For this you need a good potting soil. Make sure the bag contains only soil.

Bags labeled as potting or planting mixes are often peat based and may contain little soil. While soilless mixes can work well, they contain no nutrients, so plants growing in them need to be fertilized more frequently. Standard all-purpose houseplant soil works fine for most plants. You don't need to buy plant-specific soils.

You can purchase potting soils in 2-, 5-, 10-, and 20-quart (dry) bags. A 2-quart bag of soil is sufficient for three or four plants in 6-inch pots. A 5- or 10-quart bag will provide enough soil for at least a dozen 6-inch containers. For pots 10 inches in diameter, start with 20-quart bags.

At the nursery, test the packaged soil by squeezing the bag. It should feel soft, pliable, and slightly moist. Avoid dry, caked, or sandy soil. Look for soil that is a rich black color. Reject soil that looks old or gray; it's probably low in nutrients. Also, buy a small bag of compost (humus).

SOIL RECIPES

To make a good, all-purpose potting medium for most plants, thoroughly mix the contents of a 5-quart bag of potting soil with 2 cups of compost in a bucket.

Cacti, Succulents, and Flowering Plants. Substitute 1 cup of sharp sand for the compost. Avoid fine powdery sand, salty seashore sand, and sand with debris. For flowering plants, add 2 tablespoons of bonemeal to the basic recipe.

Gesneriads. Blend equal parts potting soil and fine-grade fir bark. Some growers prefer to raise gesneriads in a soilless mix of peat moss, perlite, and vermiculite, but you may find that the blend of soil and fir bark works better.

Orchids and Bromeliads. Grow orchids and bromeliads in fir bark, not packaged soil or a homemade mix. Of the three grades, or sizes, of bark—fine, medium, and large—medium is best. It is easy to work with, and orchids thrive in it.

Note: Soil keeps well; just store what's left over in a tightly covered container or closed plastic bag. Place the bag in a cool location.

❧ Potting Mediums ❧

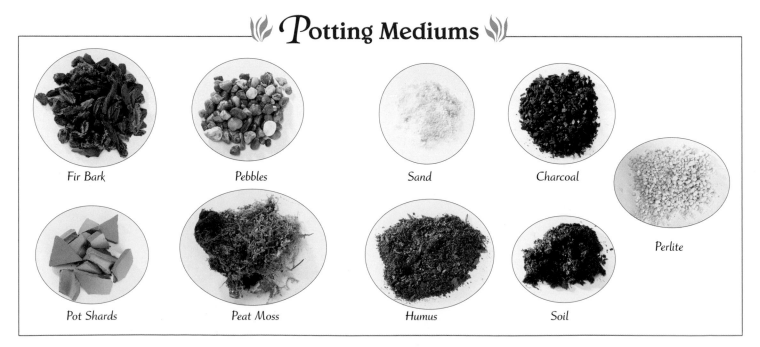

Fir Bark

Pebbles

Sand

Charcoal

Perlite

Pot Shards

Peat Moss

Humus

Soil

Potting

Many plants are sold in a mix that is mostly filler and contains little soil. If you purchase one of these, you can wait two or three weeks, if need be, before you repot the plant into good soil, but do plan to repot it eventually. Soil fillers may be sand, wood shavings, or crushed gravel, all of which furnish few if any nutrients to plants. A container that feels light, even when the potting mix is moist, probably contains mostly filler. Before you buy, ask a staffperson what kind of potting mix was used. If the plant is potted in mostly filler, gently remove as much of the original potting mix as you can. Replace it with the appropriate soil mix described under "Soil Recipes" on the preceding page.

Drainage. Be sure that any container into which you are potting has drainage holes to prevent water from standing in the container. Standing water can cause the soil to become stagnant and waterlogged. Soggy soil may eventually lead to root rot.

Sprinkle some horticultural charcoal chips in the bottom of the container to keep the soil fresh and help drainage. In small containers—6 to 10 inches in diameter—use 1 tablespoon of charcoal chips; in large containers, use 2 tablespoons. Horticultural charcoal chips are sold in boxes or bags at garden centers and nurseries. *Warning*: Do not use barbecue briquettes.

Before potting, cover the bottom of a clean container with pot shards and horticultural charcoal. The shards improve drainage, and the charcoal helps drainage and sweetens the soil.

Plants should be repotted into larger containers as they grow. Here, copper pans disguise plain pots with drainage holes. Although these plants are all about the same size, you could display a small plant on the top step in the smallest pan, a full-grown plant on the bottom in the largest container, with the other transplant sizes in between.

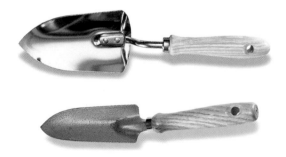

Most repotting jobs can be done with two trowels—one wide, one narrow. The wide blade is useful for scooping large amounts of soil into pots. The narrow blade works better for backfilling and working with smaller plants.

Repotting

First, choose a container. If the plant needs a larger pot, find one that is two inches deeper and wider than the original. Disinfect any containers that were previously used by soaking in a solution that is one part chlorine bleach and nine parts water. Rinse with clear water. Put a piece of mesh screen over the drainage hole so the soil doesn't wash out. Cover the screen with a layer of pot shards and then a layer of horticultural charcoal.

Note: If you are repotting a large plant or indoor tree, ask someone to help you by supporting the plant while you adjust the soil level. Two pairs of hands make it easier to properly center a large plant.

Crown

1 After removing the plant by tapping the bottom of the pot on a hard surface, grasp the plant by its crown, and gently tease it out of the pot. If the plant won't budge, slide a butter knife between the rootball and the pot, and slice around the inside of the pot.

2 Use your fingers to crumble away the old soil, and remove dead, brown roots. If the roots have taken on the shape of the container, use a fork to pull them straight or a knife to slice through them. Make three or four vertical cuts from the crown to the base.

3 Holding the plant in one hand and a trowel in the other, scoop fresh, moistened soil into the bottom of the pot. Position the plant on top of the soil. Then adjust the soil level until the crown of the plant is just above the edge of the pot.

4 Center the plant in the pot. Add soil to fill the space between the roots and the pot and to cover the roots. Press soil firmly with your thumbs to eliminate air pockets. Keep the soil level ½ inch below the pot rim to prevent overflow when watering.

5 Water the plant thoroughly in its new pot. After a few minutes, water it again. Wait 10 minutes, then discard any water sitting in the saucer. You may want to cover the plant with a plastic bag to retain moisture and lessen the chances of transplant shock.

RAISING & GROOMING

REPOTTING

Even established plants need to be repotted periodically because their roots can outgrow the containers and the soil may accumulate toxic salts from fertilizers. Established plants in containers up to 10 inches in diameter should be repotted annually. Plants in larger containers should be repotted every two years.

Plant Removal. It is easier to repot a plant when the soil is slightly dry rather than wet. Wet pots are heavy and messy to handle. As shown on the previous page, begin by tapping the side of the container several times against the edge of a countertop or table. Tap firmly but not so hard that you crack the container. That should loosen the ball of soil enough so you can remove the plant without harming the roots. Crumble away some but not all of the old soil, and trim off any dead roots.

Container Preparation. The new container should be clean. Soak a terra-cotta pot in water for a few hours before potting so that the clay will not absorb water from the soil. Disinfect reused containers by soaking them in a solution of one part chlorine bleach to nine parts water. Rinse well with clear water. Center the plant in the soil, then fill in and around the plant with soil.

Finishing Up. Firm the soil in place with your thumbs. This pressure should help to eliminate any air pockets in the soil. Roots need the air in the tiny spaces between soil particles, which are not removed when you firm the potting mix.

After you have firmed the soil, add more soil until its surface is a ½ inch from the pot rim. This reduces the probability of overflows when you water. Now tap the bottom of the container on a countertop or table again (to settle the soil), firm the soil one more time, and then water the plant thoroughly. After a few minutes, water the plant again, and discard any water standing in the saucer after another 5 or 10 minutes. Label the container with a tag that states the name of the plant and the date of repotting.

CARE AFTER REPOTTING

Repotting is a shock for plants, and newly repotted plants need a period of recuperation. Do not expose them to sun immediately because the roots are not yet up to their full strength and cannot absorb moisture readily. That's why it's important to water plants thoroughly after repotting them. A bright location that does not receive direct sun is fine. Then water plants as needed to keep the soil evenly moist but not soggy, and watch the plants for about a week to see how they are doing. If you notice that the leaves are limp (indicating insufficient water) or brown and soft at the edges (indicating too much water) adjust watering accordingly. (See "Poor Care: Symptoms and Causes," on page 97.)

Some plants have a bit of trouble recovering from repotting. Good humidity usually eases the recovery process. You can help retain humidity by covering each plant with a plastic bag. Remove the bag periodically and whenever condensation appears on the inside. You can consider the plants ready to be moved back to their regular locations when they begin to show some new growth.

Basic houseplant-care equipment includes (clockwise from left) a mister, a watering can, some twine (for staking), a sieve (for soil), and stakes and dowels (for support and to poke pilot holes for fertilizer).

A moisture meter (left) can help you determine if it's time to water. Or you can simply push your finger slightly into the soil. If the soil doesn't give, that means it's dry and in need of water.

Above: Never leave plants in standing water. If the roots stay wet, they won't get enough air. Root rot and plant death will result.

Water

Although watering is easy in itself, watering at the proper times and in the correct amounts seems to be the greatest challenge. In fact, over-watering and underwatering are the chief causes of houseplant death. Yet if you follow the guidelines below, you'll do fine.

You can water at any hour in the daytime, but avoid watering at night, which can cause fungus. Treated water out of the tap is fine for house-plants—chlorine, fluoride, and all. What is most important is the water temperature. Cold water can shock tropical houseplants, making water absorption impossible for their roots. So always use tepid, room-temperature water.

Water plants thoroughly, because an insufficient amount of water will create dry pockets in the soil; when roots reach a dry spot, they stop growing. To be sure the soil is completely saturated, water your plant, and then rewater with the excess water that drains into the saucer. Throw out the excess that drains the second

time. If standing water remains in the saucer, it will keep the soil in the pot too soggy, a condition that can cause root rot and plant death.

Keep the soil evenly moist for most house-plants. (Many cacti and succulents are exceptions, although they too need moisture.) Because large containers hold water for longer periods, you need to water plants in large containers less often. Water evaporates from terra-cotta containers faster than from glazed or plastic pots, so water plants in terra cotta more often. If the soil gives under the pressure of your finger, do not water. You can use a moisture meter, as shown at left, but using your finger can be just as reliable.

OVERHEAD WATERING

Use a metal or plastic watering can with a long spout that allows you to reach through foliage to the soil. The spout should have a *rose* (resembling a showerhead) that releases a gentle spray of water rather than a concentrated flow. Another good way to water plants is to set the pots in a sink or tub and turn on a gentle shower of tepid water. Water slowly, gently, and deeply.

Overhead watering is good because the water falls on foliage as well as the soil, and most plants like water on their leaves. However, avoid getting water on the foliage of African violets, cyclamens, gloxinias, and other plants with soft, hairy leaves. Water those plants from the bottom.

WATERING FROM THE BOTTOM

Place your pot into a dish pan, bowl, or sink of tepid water that reaches to just below the pot's rim. Let the pot absorb water until the surface soil looks and feels wet. Depending on the plant size, this may take 15 minutes to an hour. Remove the pot and allow excess water to drain.

Once a month, give all of your plants a good soaking. To do this, fill a sink or a pan with water and set the containers in the water. The water should be deep enough to reach just below pot rims. If the soil is dry, air will bubble out of the soil as water displaces it. When air bubbles no longer appear on the soil surface, remove the containers, and let the excess water drain.

Heat and Humidity

Most houseplants like average home temperatures of 70° to 78° F with a drop of 10° at night. (Exceptions are noted in the plant profiles in Part II, beginning on page 108.) The daily temperature difference helps plants manufacture sugar, which fuels their growth. Some plants, such as cyclamen and amaryllis, prefer cooler conditions. If you have cold winters and drafty windows, protect window plants by placing a sheet of material, such as poster board, between them and the windowpanes.

Humidity is a measure of the moisture in the air. Most homes have a humidity level of 30 to 40 percent, which is fine for most houseplants. Some plants, such as ferns and philodendrons, prefer higher humidity. Others, such as snake plant, prefer lower humidity.

❧ *P*lants That Dislike Dry Conditions ❧

The plants listed here prefer relative humidity of about 50 percent. If your growing area is especially dry, mist these plants occasionally, or place them on pebble trays (shown on page 76) to add some humidity in their vicinity.

Lacy maidenhair fern (*Adiantum tenerum*)
Lipstick plant (*Aeschynanthus speciosus*)
Anthurium species
Yellow plume plant, zebra plant
   (*Aphelandra squarrosa*)
Bird's nest fern (*Asplenium nidus*)
Rex begonia (*Begonia* Rex-Cultorum hybrids)
Earth star (*Cryptanthus* 'Tricolor')
Sago palm (*Cycas revoluta*)
Florist's cyclamen (*Cyclamen persicum*)
Holly fern (*Cyrtomium falcatum*)
Dendrobium species
Flame violet (*Episcia cupreata*)
Cape jasmine (*Gardenia augusta*,
   G. jasminoides)
Flame-of-the-woods (*Ixora coccinea*)
Goldfish plant (*Nematanthus* species)
Boston fern (*Nephrolepis exaltata* 'Bostoniensis')
Dancing lady orchid (*Oncidium* species)
Moth orchid (*Phalaenopsis* hybrids)
Philodendron species
Cabbage head fern, polypody
   (*Polypodium vulgare*)
Ming aralia (*Polyscias fruticosa*)

Balfour aralia (*Polyscias scutellaria* 'Balfourii')
Brake fern (*Pteris tremula*)
Moses-in-a-boat (*Rhoeo spathacea*)
Leather fern (*Rumohra adiantiformis*)
African violet (*Saintpaulia* hybrids)
Gloxinia (*Sinningia speciosa* hybrids)
Peace lily (*Spathiphyllum* species)
Cape primrose (*Streptocarpus* hybrids)
Tillandsia species

Leaf edges of this plant have turned brown and crisp in response to insufficient humidity in the room. Plants listed in this box require higher humidity levels than would be comfortable in most homes.

Plants release water through their leaves in a process called *transpiration*, and they give off moisture more quickly when the air is dry. If they lose water faster than they can replace it, their foliage becomes thin and depleted-looking. Also, the hotter the temperature, the faster air dries out.

Strong growth and firm leaves are two indications that the humidity is at the right level for your plants. Spindly growth and limp leaves usually signify too little moisture in the air. Keep houseplants away from hot radiators, hot-air vents, and drafts.

Misting. On hot summer days, mist plants lightly with water between 11:00 A.M. and 1:00 P.M. In the winter, central heating can drop humidity to an arid 20 percent. So try to keep the humidity more in balance with that of the summer months by employing a room humidifier or by misting the area around the containers and soil surface between 6:00 and 8:00 P.M. every other day. *Caution:* Do not mist the leaves of soft- or hairy-leaved plants, such as African violets, begonias, cyclamens, and gloxinias. Water can permanently damage their foliage and leave unsightly spots that won't wash off.

Misting periodically improves humidity. To protect plants from water sitting on their leaves, hold a card over the leaves, and mist the base of the plant.

Air Circulation

Good air circulation helps retard the proliferation of insects, such as mealybugs. In fact, you should let in fresh air from outdoors as much as possible. In the winter, when the air is drier inside than outside, ventilation helps maintain adequate humidity. Open a window slightly whenever the weather is not too frigid, or be sure there is sufficient ventilation near the plants. However, do not let cold air blow directly on your plants, because cold air can damage them. When it's really cold outside and impractical to open a window, use a small fan to circulate air.

In summer, air conditioning is a boon for houseplants. Most houseplants wilt in torrid weather, but air conditioning perks them up. Be sure not to let the cold air from the air conditioner blow on the plants directly. Otherwise, plant leaves may wilt or turn yellow and then fall as a result of excessive moisture loss.

Fertilizer

Plants need three major nutrients for health: nitrogen (for vigorous growth and good leaf color), phosphorus (to grow strong roots and produce seeds and fruit after flowering), and potassium, or potash (to help them absorb other nutrients and resist disease). The labels on fertilizer containers indicate the percentage of each of the three major elements, in the order listed here. For example, a 10-10-5 fertilizer contains 10 percent nitrogen (N), 10 percent phosphorus (P), and 5 percent potassium (K). The rest of the material in the bag is inert fillers, included to make it easier to give plants the right amount of fertilizer and to apply it evenly. A 10-10-10 or 20-10-10 formula is best for most houseplants, but follow guidance for specific plants given in Part II of this book.

NATURAL FERTILIZERS
Natural, or organic, plant foods are excellent sources of nitrogen, and are better than synthetic fertilizers because they add organic matter to the

Using Fertilizer Spikes

1 Use a dowel to poke a cylindrical hole into which a fertilizer spike can be placed.

2 Insert fertilizer spikes into dowel holes to furnish food to the plant gradually.

soil and their nutrients are released gradually. Cottonseed meal, fish emulsion, bloodmeal, and composted steer and cow manure are all organic nitrogen fertilizers available at nurseries and garden centers. Fish emulsion is sold in bottles and the other fertilizer types are sold in bags.

There are other organic materials that supply phosphorus and potassium, as well as organic blends that contain sources of all three nutrients. With the exception of fish emulsion, organic fertilizers do not smell bad; they have a clean earthy smell. However, organic fertilizers take more time to release their nutrients than synthetics do.

Again, there's no need to use plant foods formulated for specific plants.

SYNTHETIC FERTILIZERS

Synthetic plant foods come in the form of granules, tablets, liquids, and spikes. All are dissolved in water. Spikes are the most convenient to use. Granules are also easy because you simply sprinkle them on top of the soil and then water them in. Liquids are convenient because they allow you to feed and water at the same time. Powders can be messy. Tablets frequently do not disintegrate or spread well, and timed-release fertilizers may release too much fertilizer .

Synthetic Fertilizers

Liquid   Granule

Spike   Powder

FOUR RULES FOR HOUSEPLANT FEEDING

❧ Be sure the soil is moist.

❧ Start feeding when plants are 2 to 4 inches tall, usually about three to five weeks after seeds germinate. Because their new roots are too young to absorb nutrients, never feed seedlings.

❧ Feed only healthy plants. Sick plants cannot absorb nutrients.

❧ Do not overfertilize. Forcing a plant into growth by excessive feeding will weaken or kill it.

Trimming and Grooming

Most houseplants need trimming, grooming, and some training. (Exceptions include cacti and most succulents, orchids, and bromeliads.) Trimming involves removal of old branches to encourage fresh growth and improve overall health and vigor. Trimming also involves removal of decayed areas, which can attract fungus. Grooming involves picking off dead leaves and flowers and keeping the soil surface free of debris.

❧ Trimming Stray Branches ❧

1 Trim away errant branches to keep your plant healthy and attractive. Prune straggly branches that detract from the plant's form. To avoid tearing tissue, always cut at an angle.

2 Cover open wounds at the base of the plant with horticultural charcoal. This speeds healing by sealing cell walls and keeping disease-carrying fungus and bacteria out.

The croton (left) has grown too wide for its container. Trim the outside growth to give the plant more room. The groomed plant (right) is now properly centered and has a more pleasing shape.

Pruning shears (left) and scissors keep your houseplants neatly groomed. You can trim most of your plants with the scissors, but you'll need the pruners to cut through woody stems, such as those of the jade plant.

TRIMMING

Winter trimming could stimulate growth in dormant plants before their normal growth season. Therefore, spring is the best time to trim plants. Follow the plant's natural growth habit. For example, some plants grow in a rosette (a cluster of leaves arising from a central point). Others have a bushy, branching habit, and still others are vertical growers. Observe your plants from a distance to determine their natural growth habit.

When trimming to improve shape, remove damaged, diseased, and misshapen growth. Cut back long stems growing at odd angles using pruning scissors or shears. Use stronger pruning shears or a sharp knife to cut woody branches. After cutting, sterilize the scissors or knife to kill any disease organisms by running a flame under the blades or cleaning them with alcohol.

Cover open wounds with charcoal from a burned match to seal any open cells and keep out fungus. After you trim plants in the spring, let them rest. Keep the soil barely moist for a few weeks; then resume watering as usual.

GROOMING

Groom plants about three times a year. Get rid of any yellowed leaves and decayed flowers because they invite insects and disease.

Grooming also involves cleaning the outside of the container of any scum, algae, or other dirt with hot water and a sponge. Dirt can harbor bacteria that harms plants. Using a stiff brush, scrub off encrusted fertilizer salts.

Gently wipe the foliage of all plants, except those with fuzzy or hairy leaves, with tepid water once a month to remove insect eggs and mites.

Remove dead flower heads as soon as you notice them. Deadheading allows the plant to devote its energy to growing and staying healthy rather than producing seeds.

A spent flower has been cut from this tricolor bromeliad, leaving the red bract from which the flower stalk grew. Many bromeliads flower once, then die. Look for "pups," or offsets, from which to propagate new plants.

Resting

Like people, plants need to rest to restore their energy. Most plants rest at some time of the year. While resting, plants grow much more slowly than usual or not at all, and flowering plants stop setting buds.

Plants from different climates rest during different seasons. Plants from the Northern Hemisphere tend to rest when it's winter in that part of the world. Plants from the Southern Hemisphere, such as African violets, are more likely to rest in spring or summer north of the equator, because that's winter in their homeland. Also, for wild plants in warm climates, dormancy comes during the dry season, and growth resumes with the return of rain. Even though your houseplants may be far removed from their native habitats, their cycles of growth remain the same.

Most plants need less moisture or none at all when they are resting. The rest period is usually short, approximately three to five weeks. Many plants take a little rest after they flower. However, some plants will produce heavy foliage growth after blooming.

Your plants will indicate when they want a rest by their declining vigor. They will stop growing, and they may look a little faded or just tired. When you see the signs, gradually reduce watering, and stop feeding the plants. If you are unsure whether a plant is ready to rest or having a problem, consult its profile in Part II to see whether the plant is likely to rest at this time of year.

Seasonal & Vacation Care

The seasons influence when plants grow as well as when they rest. Most houseplants do the majority of their growing in spring and summer, so this is the time when they need the most water. Repotting of old plants is generally best done in February and March, just when they're coming out of dormancy. This way the plants have moderate weather to resume active growth. To help ready your plants for the upcoming warmer months, repot them in fresh soil, supply adequate humidity, and water regularly to keep the soil evenly moist. (See "Potting," page 65, for more information.)

Summer. During the summer months, when most plants are growing actively, give them the moisture they need. (See Part II, beginning on page 108, for information on specific plants.) Certain plants, such as columneas and some begonias, need plenty of moisture at their roots and may need daily watering. Fertilize plants that are actively growing now. Protect plants from hot sun by means of a sheer curtain or window screen. Provide good humidity and ventilation—houseplants do not thrive in a stuffy atmosphere.

When temperatures exceed 85°F, mist plants several times a day to reduce heat at their surfaces. Inspect for insects at this time of year as well. (See Chapter 7, beginning on page 96, for information on coping with insects and disease.)

All plants rest. Orchids, like many flowering plants, need time to rest between blooming periods. The orchid at left is resting, indicated by its slowed or stopped growth. Resting plants usually need less water. The orchid at right is actively growing and has sent out a bud.

Protect plants from the full strength of the sun when you first move them outside. Even geraniums, which thrive in the sun, need to be gradually acclimated. Start with plants in the shade. Then in a few days move them into diffuse light and finally into full sun.

Fall. In the fall, when days can fluctuate between warm and cool, water attentively, giving each plant the amount it needs. Plants such as gingers and some orchids are now in a semidormant state, so stop feeding them. *Remember:* Never try to force resting plants to sprout new growth. At this time, let the soil become somewhat dry but not caked between waterings.

TAKING PLANTS OUTDOORS IN SUMMER
Many houseplants enjoy and really benefit from a summer vacation outdoors. In early summer, when the nighttime temperatures no longer drop below 60°F, you can safely move tropical houseplants outdoors.

Before you move plants outside, prune those that need it. Set pots on a shady porch or patio, or in shady parts of the garden. To reduce watering frequency, you can sink the pots into the ground or even transplant them in the garden. Shade and even moisture are important because houseplants will not be able to tolerate direct summer sun.

If slugs and other soil-dwelling pests are problems, slip a piece of old pantyhose over the bottom of each pot to keep critters from crawling in through the drainage holes. Water and fertilize your houseplants—indoors and outdoors—as recommended in the plant profiles in Part II. Most plants are growing actively at this time of year.

BRINGING PLANTS INDOORS
In late summer, as days begin to grow shorter, begin preparing your houseplants for the move inside. Pinch back plants that have grown leggy. Repot plants that have outgrown their containers, giving them a larger pot and fresh soil mix. As summer draws to a close, before the weather turns cool—and certainly before there's even a remote possibility of frost—bring your houseplants indoors. Don't forget to bring in clay pots, which crack in freezing temperatures.

Northern gardeners should begin this process around Labor Day, while in the South and along the West Coast, the plants can stay outdoors until later in fall. To avoid shocking the plants, move them when the temperature outdoors is close to the temperature indoors.

Pests. Examine the plants carefully for signs of insects and disease. Especially check tender new shoots, the leaf axils (where leaves join stems), and undersides of leaves—all places where pests like to congregate.

Whiteflies have gathered on the underside of a geranium leaf. See Chapter 7, starting on page 96, for remedies.

In addition to inspecting for the pests them-selves, look for evidence of their presence, such as sticky honeydew on leaves, fine webbing in leaf axils and on shoot tips, black sooty mold, and stip-pling or chewed edges of the leaves and flowers. If you do see evidence of pests, take appropriate action as recommended in Chapter 7 before bringing the plants back indoors.

To check for soil-dwelling pests, sink each pot in a bucket of water nearly up to the rim, and let it soak for 15 minutes, as shown on page 100. Saturating the soil should drive any pests to the surface. Remove the pests, and let the pots drain.

Just to be safe, for a week or two after bring-ing the plants back indoors, keep them in a separate room from any plants that remained indoors. You don't want problems to spread to the rest of your houseplants.

YOUR VACATION

Your weekends away do not need to be a problem for your plants. To prepare your plants, thoroughly water medium-size and large containers in the morning, right before you leave. Then mist the leaves. Under these conditions, plants should stay moist for up to five days.

Up to a Week. The soil in smaller containers dries out quickly, so group small pots in a water-tight metal bin or plastic tray 5 to 6 inches deep with a 2- to 3-inch-deep layer of pebbles in the bottom. Pour water into the bin or tray until it just reaches the top of the pebbles, and then set the containers on top. Wrap and pack peat moss, paper towels, or newspaper around the outside of the pots, to within 2 inches of the rims. Dampen the wrapping, which will continue to absorb mois-ture from below and help slow the evaporation of moisture from the soil in the pots. This also helps maintain desired humidity levels above the soil, keeping small plants moist for five to seven days.

A bathtub or shower stall is a good place for small and medium-size containers while you're away. Set the containers on bricks placed in 2 to 4 inches of water, so that the water level just reaches the top of the bricks.

A pebble tray provides a good means of raising the humid-ity around plants. Rather than water each plant individually, you can simply water the pebble tray, from which the plants' roots absorb water as they need it. Be careful to keep the water level below the top of the pebbles, so the pots don't sit in water.

Gravity-powered slow waterers will take care of larger plants while you are away. Simply fill the container with water, and insert the perforated long spike into the soil. The water will gradually trickle into the soil, providing steady moisture. This device works best with moisture-loving plants.

Place a plant on bricks in a tub of water before you go on vacation. Wrap damp paper towels or peat moss around the pot to slow the evaporation from the soil to the porous pot. This contraption keeps plants moist for five to seven days.

Larger plants do best for up to a week with the use of slow waterers and capillary mats available at nurseries. After you fill one of the slow waterers and insert it into the soil, as shown below left, the container will release the water slowly.

More than a Week. If you'll be away more than a week, you can use special plant-watering devices. If your small plants are not already planted in self-watering pots, repot them into these containers. Fill the water reservoir at the bottom of each pot; wicks or other water-releasing devices supply water slowly to the soil.

Besides Water. Do not forget other environmental conditions as you prepare to leave. Consider heat and light. Do not close all the shades and blinds; plants must receive some light while you are gone. If possible, group all your plants at one or two windows, and shade the other windows.

Excessive heat can kill plants, especially in summer. If you're going to be away for a long time when it's hot, have a friend tend them or take your plants to a nursery that will plant-sit them. If you will be away for longer than a weekend at any time during the winter, set the thermostat at 65°F, which is fine for most plants.

This slow-watering plant container has a reservoir from which water is slowly drawn upward to the roots. Filling the reservoir is as easy as watering a plant.

A capillary mat provides a simple means of keeping plants watered for a few days. Capillary attraction in the soil and roots draws water upward as needed, defying gravity in a phenomenon known as *capillary action*.

CHAPTER *SIX*

Propagating Houseplants

*P*urchasing houseplants is just one way to acquire them. Once you have a few plants and have learned how to deal with their idiosyncrasies, you will undoubtedly want to have more plants.

You can get lots of new plants basically free by growing them from seed or by propagating them through other methods from plants you already have. A handy table on page 94, "Propagation Methods & Hints," lists methods that work best for specific plants. The table also includes cultivation tips to help you increase your chances of success. Propagating your own plants is fun: It gives you a wonderful sense of creation and saves money, and it is not difficult.

Propagating plants from stolons, or runners, as shown trailing from this spider plant, is one of many easy options for increasing your plant collection.

Propagating with Seed

Starting houseplants from seed takes time and patience, but it's worth it. There is a sense of accomplishment in growing your own plants from scratch.

CONTAINERS

Seed can be sown in all sorts of containers, ranging from special terra-cotta pots, peat pots, and seed pellets to recyclables, including egg cartons, plastic storage boxes, and aluminum trays from frozen foods. Any container you use for growing seed should be 4 to 5 inches deep, with drainage holes in the bottom; you can use an ice pick to poke out drainage holes.

Terra-Cotta Pots. Terra-cotta, or clay, pots are attractive, inexpensive, and easy to use.

Peat Pots. To use peat pots, which are made of compressed peat, soak the pots in water, fill them with soil, and insert a few seeds. When leaves appear, transplant the pots into larger containers, making sure the rims of the peat pots are completely buried. It's a good idea to tear their sides when transplanting to ensure that roots can grow.

Peat containers, available round or square, can be filled with sterile medium. They are equally suited to starting seeds and rooting cuttings, as shown here. Seed pellets, which look like biscuits in a tray, are used to start seeds. (Also see photos at right.)

Transplanting with peat pots reduces shock by minimizing damage to tender new roots.

Seed Pellets. Seed pellets, or disks, are even easier to use: Simply add water and insert the seed. The pellet expands and becomes the container. When leaves appear, transplant the plant along with the expanded pellet into a larger container with soil. Again, tear or cut the sides of the pellet to ensure that the roots can easily reach surrounding soil.

Seed pellets (top) expand when watered. The pellets become containers. **Above**: Use a pair of tweezers or a folded piece of paper to place the seeds in the pellet.

Recycled Containers. If you use a recycled container to start seeds, be sure to disinfect and rinse it thoroughly—containers for seed starting need to be clean. Recycled containers are less convenient than peat pots or pellets, but they're free.

Covered Units. You can purchase special seed-starting and propagation units that come with their own covers. Some of them also supply bottom heat. They are available by mail order.

GROWING MEDIUM
Use a sterile medium, such as disinfected soil, vermiculite, perlite, sand, sphagnum moss, or a combination that drains well and retains moisture. Or use a commercial seed-starting mix. Garden soil and old potting soil may contain disease

Square peat pots separate easily.

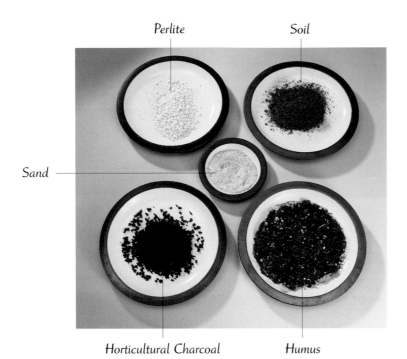

Perlite

Soil

Sand

Horticultural Charcoal

Humus

A satisfactory houseplant medium contains the following ingredients: soil, humus, horticultural charcoal, sand, perlite.

organisms and a fungus that causes "damping-off," which kills seedlings. Fill the containers with the soil mix you wish to use, to about ½ inch from the top. Then spray the medium gently with water until it is moist, but not soggy, all the way through. If the seeds are large, 1⁄16 to ¼ inch, press them about ¼ inch into the medium.

If the seeds are too small for you to handle individually, sprinkle them on top of the medium, and then scatter a thin layer of sterile soil over them. Spray the medium again, very gently, to moisten the top layer of soil, and place the container in a shady spot where the temperature is a warm 72° to 78°F.

HUMIDITY

To increase humidity, make a little greenhouse over the container. To do this, prop a layer of plastic wrap or a plastic bag over a framework of four sticks inserted into each corner of the soil. The greenhouse effect will retain enough humidity to keep the growing medium moist, which is essential. Check the medium every day to be sure the seed is not receiving too much

moisture. If that is the case, the inside of the plastic will be wet. If so, remove the plastic for a few hours each day so that air can circulate around the seedlings. If the medium feels dry, mist it with water.

TEMPERATURE

The correct temperature is crucial for germination. Low-voltage heating cables laid in the soil are excellent because they maintain a constant gentle temperature of 70° to 78°F. Heating cables are available at many nurseries and garden centers. Or if you have an older refrigerator, place the seed tray on top; the warm air from the coils behind the unit will rise to the top, providing bottom

Seed-starting kits include a tray and a clear cover to retain moisture. **Top**: The seed has germinated and the seed leaves (cotyledons) are up. **Above**: True leaves have appeared.

heat. Never place containers on top of a radiator because the heat cycles from too high to too low.

GERMINATION

Depending on the plant, seed takes several days to several months to germinate. When the first tiny green shoots appear, supply more air by removing the plastic tent for most of the day. The first pair of seed leaves, or *cotyledons*, are generally round or oval. True leaves are usually the second set of leaves a seedling develops and have the mature plant's characteristic leaf shape. Discard the tent when true leaves sprout. Give the seedlings more light, and be sure that through the entire germination period the growing medium remains uniformly moist but not wet.

❧ Germinating Seeds ❧

1 Fill a clean plastic tray with sterile medium. Use a piece of wood to make rows.

2 Sow seed according to directions on the seed packet, using a folded sheet of paper.

3 Cover seed lightly with soil, using a trowel. This step is optional.

4 Trickle water slowly over the seedbed until the medium is evenly moist.

5 Cover with plastic to retain humidity. Remove once a day to allow some air in.

6 When seedlings have two to four leaves, move to a 2-inch pot.

TRANSPLANTING & REPOTTING

When seedlings display their true leaves, remove weaker plants with a pair of tweezers, or nudge them out of the medium with a pencil to give the sturdier seedlings more room to grow. Work carefully to avoid injuring the delicate roots of nearby seedlings.

Transplanting. When the plants are large enough to be handled, remove them from their starter container, and plant each one in a separate, 2-inch pot in a sterile, packaged houseplant soil. Handle them by the seed leaves, not by the true leaves, stems, or roots. Young seedlings are delicate, and it's easy to damage the stems or true leaves, which could interfere with future growth. Think of the cotyledons as baby teeth. They are temporary and will soon be replaced by the true leaves.

As you transplant the seedlings, be careful not to disturb the rootball. And be sure to plant them in room-temperature soil and to water them with warm water. Cold water can shock the plant; hot water will scald it.

Next, put the newly planted pots in a terrarium or other moisture-retaining enclosure for several days to allow the plants to recover from transplant shock. Do not let the soil become overly moist or overly dry. Check the moisture level by poking your finger into the soil. When the soil doesn't give and feels dry below the surface, it's time to water. Keep the soil evenly moist.

Repotting. When the seedlings are a few inches tall, repot them again. The ideal container diameter for most young houseplants is 3 to 4 inches. Later, when the plant outgrows this container, you can repot it in a larger pot. For this more permanent potting, use a packaged soil mixed with humus or sand, as described under "Potting" on page 65.

Transplanting can occcur when seedlings are sturdy enough to handle. This basil seedling has two distinct types of leaves: Its first leaves, or cotyledons, and the second set of leaves, or true leaves. The seed leaves are round and the true leaves are long and oval, resembling the leaves of the mature plant. Use a pencil to gently nudge the seedling out of the pot. Always handle seedlings by their cotyledons, never by the true leaves or stem, which can easily be damaged.

Repot plants when they outgrow their containers (right). Transplant seedlings into 2-inch pots, then into 3-or 4-inch pots, and later into larger pots. The plant shown here at different stages is schefflera, not basil.

Vegetative Propagation

There are other ways to start plants besides planting seed. Vegetative methods of propagation produce new plants from plant parts. These new plants are genetically identical to the parent.

Vegetative propagation is the only way to reproduce hybrids, which do not "come true" (meaning they cannot be exactly duplicated) from seed. For the most part, vegetative propagation is easier and faster than starting plants from seed.

PLANTING OFFSETS AND RUNNERS

Among the simplest ways of producing new plants is to divide offsets and runners from the parent plant. Many plants produce offsets, which are small duplicate plants that grow from buds at the crown of the parent plant. Other plants produce aboveground runners, called *stolons*, from which tiny plants emerge.

Plants such as agaves and bromeliads and some gesneriads bear offsets at the base of the plant. When these offsets are 2 to 4 inches tall, cut them off and root them in soil.

Plants, such as spider plants and flame violets, bear runners. To produce new plants from either of these, cut the connecting stem, as shown below, and insert the new plant in soil where it will root and grow. Another method is to plant the baby plants in pots of soil and let them form roots before you sever them from the parent plant, as shown above right.

You can propagate runners by placing the young plant in a prepared pot of soil in a semi-layering method. Leave the runner attached to the mother plant for a few weeks, then cut it from the parent.

❧ Planting Runners ❧

1 Select a healthy plant that has runners or offsets. Cut off the small plantlets using a sterile knife.

2 Dip the cutting in hormone powder, which speeds rooting.

3 Place the runner cutting in fresh soil in a small pot, and water.

Propagating by Division

Division is a method of separating a plant that forms a clump of stems into two or more smaller plants. This is a good technique to use when you don't want to put a plant in a bigger pot. (See pages 94–95 for suitable plants.)

The first step in dividing a plant is to remove it from its pot. See "Repotting," page 66, for information on unpotting plants. Next, shake some soil from the roots so that you can see the crown, the point at which the roots meet the stem. Look for natural divisions in the clump of stems. Pull the plant apart into sections, or use a sterile sharp knife to cut it apart where the natural divisions occur. Sterilize your knife by passing it over a flame or dipping it in rubbing alcohol. Make sure each division has ample roots to support the top growth.

After dividing the plant, gently tease away more soil from the roots. Cut away any roots that are dead (brown at the tips) or damaged. Immediately pot each plant in fresh soil so that the roots do not dry out. It isn't necessary to dip roots into water first if you repot divisions right away.

If the plant grows from tubers, such as dahlias or tuberous begonias, or from rhizomes, such as rhizomatous begonias, divide it by cutting apart the clumps of swollen roots. To propagate orchids, divide the pseudobulbs, the thick stems that arise from the rhizome at intervals. Try to give each division at least three pseudobulbs.

Another way to propagate plants by division is to place them in a tall glass of water. Keep the glass on a bright but not sunny window ledge, and change the water weekly.

To increase the humidity, put a plastic bag loosely over the division (see page 86). When the division shows one- or two-inch long roots, remove it from the water.

Dip the newly formed roots into hormone powder. Plant the rooted division in a two- or three-inch container of sterile potting medium. Keep the soil evenly moist and put the cutting in a warm place (between 75° to 80°F.)

Dividing Most Plants

1 Grasp an overgrown potted plant at the bottom, and locate natural divisions in the plant by viewing them from the top.

2 Remove the plant from the pot, and then gently pry apart each division.

3 Fill new pots with fresh soil and plant one division per pot.

✿ Dividing a Bromeliad ✿

1 This crowded bromeliad needs to be divided. Remove part of the plant by cutting through the rootstock using a sterile knife.

2 After lining a clean pot with shards to provide adequate drainage, fill the pot with fir bark or a soil-and-bark mixture.

3 Firm the potting medium

✿ Dividing an Orchid ✿

1 To divide an established orchid, grasp part of the plant, and cut using a sterile knife, leaving at least three pseudobulbs per division.

2 Fill the new pot with fir bark or soil-and-bark mix.

✿ Dividing an African Violet ✿

1 To divide an African violet, grasp the plant with two hands. Then gently pull the root mass apart.

2 Transplant each division into a new pot filled with soil.

$\mathscr{P}$ropagating with Cuttings

TAKING TIP CUTTINGS

Stem, or "tip," cuttings and leaf cuttings produce new plants exactly like the parent. To take a tip cutting, remove a stem 3 or 4 inches from the tip. Then cut below a leaf node, and remove bottom leaves. For most plants, spring is the best time for this. (See pages 94–95 for suitable plants.)

Plants with little top growth and woodier stems, such as ti plant (*Cordyline terminalis*), can be reproduced by rooting sections of stems in a warm, moist soil mix.

To root stems, fill a container with 3 or 5 inches of medium. Dip the cut end of the stem

Taking Tip Cuttings

1 Select a healthy overgrown plant. Pinch stems to remove cuttings, or use a sterile knife.

2 On a wooden board, prepare the tip cuttings for potting.

3 Dip ends of cuttings in commercial rooting hormone powder.

4 Place each cutting in a separate pot. Insert wooden sticks, and place a plastic bag loosely over the cuttings. Keep the plastic loose so air circulates within the plastic tent. Remove the tent whenever condensation develops. Keep the soil moist. Roots will grow, and the plants will be ready for potting in larger containers in two to three weeks.

in rooting hormone powder, and insert the cutting about 2 inches into the medium. Cover the container with a clear plastic tent to provide the high humidity that cuttings need to form roots.

Keep the growing medium evenly moist, and set the container in a warm, 75°F, low-lit location. Tug gently on the cutting every few days to see if it has roots. When the plant resists your gentle tug, roots have formed. Transplant the rooted cutting into a 3-inch container of sterile growing medium, as described on page 79.

🌿 Taking a Sansevieria Leaf Cutting 🌿

1 To propagate a sansevieria from leaves, use a sharp sterile knife to remove a leaf at its base.

2 On a wooden board, cut the leaf into 2-inch sections.

3 Fill a pot with soil, and insert the sections about halfway down into the soil. Note: Insert the tip section cut side down. Then water and keep the soil moist.

LEAF CUTTINGS

Like tip cuttings, leaves and pieces of leaves can be cut and inserted into pots of soil to root and produce new plants. The new plants grow from the leaf blade itself. (See pages 94–95 for suitable plants.)

First, remove a healthy leaf still attached to a portion of stem. Then you can either cut the leaf into pieces or use the whole leaf. Cover the leaf with a clear transluscent cover. If you don't have a commercial cover, you can use a plastic bag or an inverted glass jar. Place the covered container in a warm, low-lit spot for a few weeks.

As shown on the next page, you can place certain leaf cuttings horizontally on vermiculite. Rex begonias, kalanchoes, and African violets can all be propagated this way. After cutting across the leaf veins in several places on the underside of the leaves, lay the leaves—right side up—flat on the vermiculite. Rooting plantlets will soon appear along the cuts and will at first obtain their nourishment from the mother leaf. When you can handle the new plants easily, cut them from the parent leaf, and pot each one separately in soil.

❧ Taking Leaf-Section Cuttings ❧

1 You can make new plants from pieces of leaves. After removing a leaf from an established plant, place it on a wood board and cut the leaf into triangular pieces. Multiple cuttings can be taken from one leaf as long as each has veins.

2 Insert the pointed ends of the cuttings halfway into a sterile medium in a tray. Lightly water the cuttings, and place a plastic cover over them. In a few weeks, after the leaves emerge, put the new plants into individual pots.

Taking Whole-Leaf Cuttings

1 Select a healthy leaf and, using a sterile knife, cut it from the base of the plant. Be sure to keep the stem attached.

2 Place the leaf upside down. After removing the stem, use a sharp knife to cut across the veins on the underside of the leaf.

3 Place the leaves upside down in the potting tray, and pin each leaf to the medium with a hair pin.

4 Gently water the medium, but avoid wetting the leaves. Cover them with a dome to retain adequate humidity.

5 In a few weeks, when baby leaves emerge, remove the dome. Place the tray in a warm spot, and keep the medium moist.

6 Transfer young plants to pots filled with fresh soil. Young plants generally like snug quarters.

Propagating by Air Layering

Plants with woody stems that tend to grow lanky and lose their lower leaves with age, such as rubber trees and dieffenbachias, are best propagated by air layering. With this method, you need to wait six to nine months for new roots to form.

Don't throw away the old plant. Cut the stem back just above a bud. Place the plant in a warm spot, and keep the soil moist. In a few weeks several new shoots will emerge. Good candidates for air layering include dieffenbachias, dracaenas, ficus, and swiss cheese plant.

1 Remove the lower leaves on the main stem. Using a sharp knife, cut on a diagonal partially through the stem. Note that the cut is made directly below a leaf node. Place a toothpick in the cut to keep it open.

2 Place a plastic tent around the open cut, and then fill with moist sphagnum moss. Tie one end shut. Be sure the moss forms a compact mass around the cut before tying the other end of the plastic.

3 When you can see roots forming within the plastic ball, sever the stem at the base.

4 Remove the plastic, and then place the rooted air-layered stem in fresh soil in a pot. Water thoroughly.

Propagating Bulbs

A rhizome, or swollen root, is placed in soil and partially covered before being watered. Curcuma (below) grows from a rhizome.

Place curcuma in bright light, and continue to water. A new plant will emerge after a few weeks. Bloom occurs when the plant matures after a few months.

Plants that grow from bulblike structures (including bulbs, corms and rhizomes) are easy to propagate; they already contain all necessary nutrients to produce a new plant. You just need to provide water and warmth. After the plants bloom, allow the foliage to gradually turn yellow and die by cutting back on water; this allows the bulb to gather food through its leaves to be stored for the next year's growth. Remove the leaves after they die, and place the pot in a cool (60°F), dry place and keep the soil barely moist. In the spring, repot the bulb in fresh soil.

Planting Bulbs

1 Plant healthy bulbs in a mix of equal parts potting soil and sterile medium, such as vermiculite.

2 Water moderately, and place the container in a warm area with bright light but not direct sun.

You can add color to your indoor garden during the drab days of winter by forcing bulbs into bloom. Forcing causes bulbs to flower before they normally would outdoors.

Start the process in autumn. Buy the best-quality bulbs you can find. When you pick out bulbs, examine them thoroughly. You want bulbs that are firm and solid, with no mold, soft spots, or physical damage. Store tender bulbs in a cool location with good air circulation. Store hardy bulbs in the refrigerator. Even hardy bulbs will not survive in the freezer. Lacking the insulating protection of soil or snow that they receive when planted outside, bulbs will succumb to frostbite.

It takes 8 to 12 weeks to force bulbs into bloom, so plan ahead. Plant your bulbs in 5- to 6-inch-diameter pots filled with a well-drained, porous medium such as a mix of equal parts potting soil, peat moss, and sharp sand. Use pots with drainage holes. A conventional 6-inch pot will accommodate three daffodils or hyacinths or five to six tulips. Smaller bulbs, such as crocuses or netted iris, can be forced in a 5-inch bulb pan (a pot that is wider than high).

Pots. Scrub the pots with a stiff brush to remove dirt, algae, and salt buildup. Soak them in a solution of one part chlorine bleach to nine parts water. Rinse well. Soak clay pots overnight in clear water so the walls will not draw moisture from the potting mix after the bulbs are planted.

Special bulb-forcing pots allow the bulb shoots to grow out the sides. These pots give the bulbs plenty of fresh air, which they need.

Planting. Most bulbs can be planted with the tips exposed. Don't bury them completely unless noted in the table at right. Set them so that the soil level will be about ½ inch below the rim of the pot. Plant as many bulbs as will fit in the pot, leaving about 1½ inches of space between them. Water to thoroughly moisten the soil mix. Cover the pots to keep out light.

Location. Place pots of hardy bulbs in a cold location with temperatures of 35° to 45° F. If you expect below-freezing temperatures, insulate the pots by covering them with shredded leaves or a blanket. During the cold period, the roots will grow. Place pots of tender bulbs, such as florist's anemone, in a cool location, where the temperature is 45° to 55°F.

Water and Light. Check the pots weekly to be sure the soil remains moist but not wet. Do not fertilize. When the chilling period is over, bring the pots into bright light to produce flowers. Most bulbs do best in a bright but rather cool location indoors. Water to keep the soil evenly moist.

To layer bulbs for forcing, put large bulbs such as daffodils near the bottom of the pot. Cover them with soil. Add smaller bulbs on top and cover them with a layer of soil.

Tips for Forcing Bulbs

Name	Temp./Weeks of Cold	Notes
Florist's anemone *Anemone coronaria*	45–50°F for 6–8 weeks	Soak tubers before planting until they're soft enough to dent with a fingernail.
Dutch crocus *Crocus* cultivars	35-45°F for 8 weeks	Water sparingly until plants are fully grown. Then keep evenly moist.
Freesia *Freesia* cultivars	50°F for 8 weeks	Plant corms deep enough to just barely, but completely, cover them. Plants need 10°F temperature drop at night.
Hyacinth *Hyacinthus orientalis*	45–50°F for 8 weeks	Easiest of the hardy bulbs to force; can be forced in water or soil.
Netted iris *Iris reticulata* *Iris danfordiae*	35–45°F for 8 weeks	Plant 2–3 inches deep and 2–3 inches apart.
Corn lily *Ixia* cultivars	50°F for 8 weeks	After forcing, rest bulbs over the summer, and force again next season.
Enchantment lily *Lilium* 'Enchantment'	60°F for 3–4 weeks	As plant grows, feed monthly with an all-purpose fertilizer.
Paperwhite narcissus *Narcissus papyraceus*	No cold period needed	Can be forced in soil or a pebble-filled bowl of water. Practically foolproof.
Narcissus and daffodils *Narcissus* cultivars	35–45°F for 12 weeks	Plants do best in cool temperatures of 60–65°F.
Persian buttercup *Ranunculus asiaticus*	50°F for 8 weeks	Soak tubers before planting until they're soft enough to dent with a fingernail.
Tulips *Tulipa* cultivars	35–45°F for 12 weeks	Plant bulbs with tips ½ inch deep. As plants grow, give them bright light but no direct sun.

PLANT	METHOD	HINTS
Abutilon × *hybridum* (flowering maple)	Tip cuttings, seed	Needs ample humidity
Acalypha hispida (chenille plant)	Tip cuttings	Needs good humidity
Adiantum tenerum (maidenhair fern)	Division	Easy
Aechmea species (vase plant)	Offsets	Easy
Aeschynanthus speciosus (lipstick plant)	Tip cuttings, runners	Subject to damping-off
Aglaonema commutatum (Chinese evergreen)	Division, stem or tip cuttings	Easy
Aloe species	Offsets	Easy
Anthurium andraeanum (flamingo flower)	Division	Dust ends of cutting in hormone powder
Aphelandra squarrosa (zebra plant)	Tip cuttings, seed	Cut plants yearly to prevent leggy growth
Asparagus densiflorus (foxtail fern)	Division	Easy
Aspidistra elatior (cast iron plant)	Division	Easy
Asplenium nidus (bird's nest fern)	Division	Easy
Begonia, all types	Leaf cuttings, division	Needs ample humidity
Billbergia species	Offsets	Easy
Calathea makoyana (peacock plant)	Division	Subject to damping-off
Caryota mitis (fishtail palm)	Division, offsets	Slow growing
Cattleya cultivars	Division	Easy
Chlorophytum comosum (spider plant)	Runners	Grow in water
Cissus discolor (begonia vine)	Stem cuttings	Easy
Clivia miniata (kaffir lily)	Division	Divide in late summer
Codiaeum variegatum var. *pictum* (croton)	Stem cuttings, seed	Easy
Coleus cultivars (painted nettle)	Tip cuttings, seed	Needs ample humidity
Columnea species	Tip cuttings	Sometimes unsuccessful
Cordyline terminalis (ti plant)	Division	Easy
Cryptanthus species	Offsets	Easy
Dieffenbachia amoena (dumbcane)	Tip cuttings or air layering	Layering best
Dizygotheca elegantissima (false aralia)	Tip cuttings	Difficult to start
Dracaena species	Division	Easy to start
Epipremnum aureum (pothos)	Tip cuttings	Very easy
Episcia species	Stem or leaf cuttings	Needs ample humidity

Note: *See Part II for propagation methods for plants not listed here.*

PLANT	METHOD	HINTS
Euphorbia milii var. *splendens* (crown-of-thorns)	Tip cuttings	Easy
Euphorbia pulcherrima (poinsettia)	Stem cuttings*	Will root in water
Ficus species (fig or rubber plant)	Air layering	Usually successful
Guzmania lingulata	Offsets	Easy
Gynura aurantiaca (purple velvet plant)	Tip cuttings	Temperamental
Heliconia species	Division	Easy
Hoya carnosa (wax plant)	Tip cuttings	Difficult
Kalanchoe blossfeldiana (starfire kalanchoe)	Seed	Difficult
Maranta species (prayer plant)	Division	Subject to damping-off
Medinilla magnifica (pink grape plant)	Stem cuttings	Difficult
Monstera deliciosa (Swiss cheese plant)	Stem cuttings, air layering	Layering usually successful
Neoregelia carolinae	Offsets	Easy
Nephrolepis exaltata (Boston fern)	Division	Easy
Oncidium species (dancing lady orchid)	Division	Easy
Paphiopedilum species (lady slipper orchid)	Division	Easy
Pelargonium cultivars (geranium)	Stem cuttings	Dust ends of cutting in hormone powder
Peperomia species	Stem or leaf cuttings	Easy
Philodendron species	Tip or stem cuttings	For most types, just place cutting in water
Polypodium vulgare (polypody)	Division	Easy
Saintpaulia cultivars (African violet)	Leaf cuttings	Easy
Sansevieria trifasciata (snake plant)	Division; leaf cuttings	Division easy
Schefflera actinophylla (umbrella tree)	Tip cuttings	A bit difficult
Scindapsus	Tip cuttings	Easy
Spathiphyllum species (peace lily)	Division	Easy
Streptocarpus rexii (cape primrose)	Leaf cuttings, division	Very easy
Syngonium podophyllum	Stem cuttings	Easy
Vriesea species	Offsets	Easy
Zantedeschia	Separate bulbs	Easy
Zebrina pendula	Tip cuttings	Will root in water

***Note:** *Wear gloves when handling* Euphorbia *because the sap can cause a rash.*

chapter
SEVEN

Problems: Symptoms & Cures

*T*oday, improved growing conditions at suppliers increase the likelihood that the plants you bring home will be pest- and disease-free. Pest and disease problems are most likely to develop when plants are growing in unfavorable conditions or are weakened by poor care. Because inappropriate growing conditions lead to stressed plants that are more susceptible to pest infestation and disease, the best defense is to provide optimal growing conditions. Make sure your plants receive the right amount of light, moisture, humidity, and fertilizer and that the indoor temperatures are suitable for each plant.

Inspecting for Symptoms. You can avoid serious problems by inspecting plants for signs of disease or insects. To detect insects, examine the tops and undersides of leaves. Examine new shoots for distorted growth and for yellowing or discolored leaves. Look for webbing in leaf axils, stickiness on stems, and insects themselves.

Most diseases are caused by either bacteria or fungi, both of which enter a plant through minute wounds or natural openings such as leaf pores. Once inside the plant, bacteria and fungi multiply rapidly and start to break down plant tissue.

When a plant shows evidence of insects or disease, isolate and treat it for at least a month to contain the problem. In the case of an insect infestation, wait a few more weeks before returning the plant to its usual location; this is to ensure that no eggs are hatching new generations of pests. Also see "Insect Control," on page 100 and "Plant Diseases," on page 102.

Use a magnifying glass to inspect your plants for insects. Look closely at the tops and bottoms of leaves.

Poor Care: Symptoms & Possible Causes

Plants that are yellowing and losing leaves aren't necessarily succumbing to a disease or being attacked by pests. Poor care, or cultural practices, may be to blame. Plants showing physical problems may need soil with better drainage, a different watering schedule, increased humidity, or just more fresh air. When there are multiple possible causes, change just one condition at a time to isolate the problem.

SYMPTOM	POSSIBLE CAUSES
Leaves are spotted brown or yellow	Heat too high; humidity too low; not enough fresh air; soil too dry or too wet
Leaves have yellow or white rings	Water too cold (requires room-temperature water)
Leaves drop	Temperature extreme; water too cold; humidity too low
Leaves are pale, growing weakly	Light insufficient; heat too high; too much fertilizer
Plant grows slowly	Soil drainage poor; plant resting
Buds drop	Humidity too low; temperature extreme; shock from draft
Plant collapses	Temperature extreme; root rot from poor drainage
Leaves are dry and crumbling	Heat too high; humidity too low
Leaves wilt	Soil too dry; heat too high
Stems are leggy and weak; leaves are sparse	Light insufficient

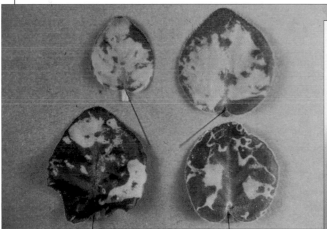

Spotted leaves (above) suggest various potential problems: heat too high, humidity too low, not enough fresh air, or soil too dry or too wet. Change the conditions one at a time to be sure of the cause. **Right**: Lack of water and humidity or excessive heat, or both, have caused this plant to wilt. **Far right**: Insufficient light caused this plant to reach awkwardly toward the sun and grow leggy stems with sparse leaves.

Wilting Plant

Leggy, Reaching Plant

Pests

Insects may be able to gain a foothold on your plants, despite good cultural practices. They can ride indoors with new plants, or they may lie dormant in the soil until the conditions are right for them to emerge. Ongoing inspection and good growing conditions will help you prevent a few insects from becoming a major pest problem.

If you discover harmful insects on your plants, try physical remedies first, such as picking them off by hand or wiping them off with a damp cloth.

If these benign physical methods don't work, try the home remedies described on pages 100–101. Before you resort to commercial insecticides, consider throwing out the plant and replacing it. Try insecticides only as a last resort, and be sure to follow label instructions carefully.

Hint: To keep treasured plants going, continually propagate them. Then, if an older plant should develop a problem, you will still have its offpring.

Scale are tiny, oval-shaped, soft-bodied immobile insects protected by a hard shell. These insects suck plant sap, leaving plants sticky and causing yellowing.

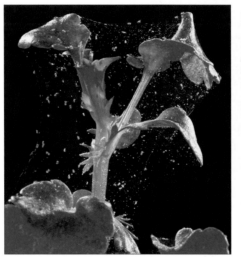

Spider mites are tiny arachnids that suck the sap from leaves or flowers, leaving plants with yellow blotches and causing leaf loss. Look for spider mite webbing between leaves and stems. These pests love hot, dry conditions.

Whiteflies are tiny, mothlike insects with greenish larvae that suck leaves, causing yellowing and leaf loss. Adult whiteflies flutter around like snowflakes when an infested plant is shaken.

Ants themselves do no damage, but some herd aphids for the honeydew they excrete and may transport plant disease. **Aphids**, as shown here, are one of the most bothersome plant pests. These green, black, or red insects pierce stems, leaves, and buds, leaving plants weak with stunted or deformed leaves and blooms. They often cluster in leaf axils, along stems, and on the undersides of leaves.

Mealybugs are small, white, cottonlike insects that form colonies and destroy plant tissue. Infestation can lead to plant wilt, yellowing, and leaf loss. Look for mealybugs along tender new shoots and in leaf axils.

Beneficials

Not all plant insects are bad. Some are beneficial in the indoor garden and on houseplants that seasonally go outside. Though few people may want insects inside their homes, ladybird beetles (ladybugs) and their larvae, lacewings and their larvae, tachinid and syrphid flies, and praying mantids all eat insects that feast on houseplants. Beneficial insects may hitchhike into your home on new plants or gain access through open doors or windows. If you find beneficials on your houseplants, you may prefer to move them outdoors, but don't kill them.

Larva

Adult

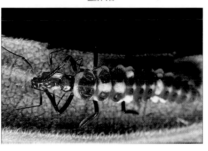

Ladybird beetles (ladybugs) are usually bright orange-red with black spots or black with red spots. They eat the eggs and young of aphids, scale, and other soft-bodied insects. Ladybug larvae somewhat resemble tiny, flat alligators. They are even more voracious than adults.

Tachinid (top) and **syrphid flies** are members of separate families with larvae that prey on aphids and scale. Although this tachinid resembles a bee and this syrphid resembles a yellow jacket, neither stings. Some family members instead resemble houseflies.

Praying mantids, so called because of their "praying" stance, dine on many plant insects, including beneficials. Depending on the species, an adult praying mantid, may range in size from 1 to 4 inches.

Insect Control

Insects tend to attack plants that are growing in less-than-optimal conditions. Houseplants are sometimes attacked by pests that like the hot, dry conditions found in many homes during the winter. To prevent problems, provide plants with fresh air, increase room humidity, and keep the temperature between 65° and 75°F. Occasionally open a window a bit. Also invest in a humidifier, and lower your thermostat a few degrees.

Try to keep insects from entering your home on a new plant. Examine new plants carefully. Insects hiding in soil or on the undersides of leaves can be difficult to see. As a precaution, soak newly purchased houseplants in a tub of water up to the pot rim for a few minutes. This will bring insects in the soil to the surface so you can dispose of them. If some of your houseplants spend the summer outdoors, check them carefully before bringing them back inside.

Soak new plants in water to bring insects to the surface.

Inspect all your plants regularly for signs of insects. Some insects have preferred locations. For example, mealybugs and aphids lurk in leaf axils and on the undersides of leaves. Thrips inhabit soil, and scale generally cling to stems at the lower part of a leaf.

Plants with thin, delicate leaves, such as calatheas, are more susceptible to insects than thick-leaved plants. Succulents are seldom attacked by critters because their leaves are thick and tough skinned.

HOME REMEDIES

Even with the best of care, the strongest plants may occasionally be attacked by insects. Often the best defenses against houseplant critters are traditional home remedies. Always test any treatment on a few leaves before applying it to the whole plant. Before panicking and resorting to harsh chemicals, try physical controls or the home remedies described below. Or, if you have a heavily infested plant, it's often better to dispose of it in a sealed plastic bag.

Hand Picking. If you see insects, use a toothpick or tweezers to remove them, and then destroy them by dropping them into a container of soapy water. Remove any dead or diseased leaves. Clean your tweezers and scissors with rubbing alcohol, or pass them over a flame so you don't inadvertently carry the insects from one part of the plant to another.

Damp Wiping. Wipe plant leaves, both top and bottom, with a cloth dampened with clear water. This eliminates many insect eggs and discourages pests that like dry conditions.

Water Spray. To dislodge a small number of pests from a plant, try a simple blast from your kitchen sink sprayer or bathroom shower head. Also start misting your plants every other day. This may not sound like a high-tech solution, but spraying plants regularly will deter many insects that prefer dry conditions. Mist plants at a sink or in a shower so

Swab tobacco tea on leaves to get rid of scale or mealybugs.

controls encourages pest populations to develop higher resistance. (Everyone knows about cockroaches; they have evolved such resistance to insecticides that they are jokingly referred to as the only family likely to survive a nuclear blast.) Always follow the package directions, and always use these products with caution.

Rubbing Alcohol. To kill aphids, mealybugs, and scale, dab them with a cotton swab soaked with rubbing alcohol. Repeat applications every two to three days. This method takes a little time, but it is effective. Alcohol sprays may be efficient on insects but are not recommended for plants. Covering the whole leaf can cause damage to the plant tissues.

Tobacco Tea. Tobacco is just as bad for insects as it is for humans. Use it to rid your plants of scale, which can be tough to eliminate. To make the tea, steep tobacco in water for several days. Dip a cotton swab in the tea, and dab the insects. *Caution:* Keep this highly toxic tea in a sealed jar out of reach of pets and children.

you can thoroughly drench the plant without damaging your furniture or floors.

Soap Treatment. Clean more heavily infested plants with soapy water. Use a mild dishwashing liquid that has no whiteners, fragrance, or other additives. Squirt 2 teaspoonfuls into 1 gallon of water, and carefully wash the plant. Pay special attention to the undersides of leaves and the base of the leaf where it attaches to the stem. If this seems too tedious, cover the soil with aluminum foil, hold the plant by its base, and plunge the foliage into the soapy water. This soapy solution will also deter aphids and mealybugs when applied directly on them.

As a preventive measure, spray plants once a week with a solution of soap and water. Rinse any plant washed with soapy water well using warm water 10 minutes after the soap treatment.

Insecticidal Soap. If a larger number of insects is present, try an insecticidal soap. Made of sodium or potassium salts, insecticidal soaps are effective against many household pests and are not harmful to people or pets if they are used at the recommended dosage. Still, it's best to restrict your use of these products. Frequent use of chemical

Sticky traps are used to catch flying insects such as whitefly that have attacked houseplants.

Insecticide Use & Storage

Always follow the manufacturer's directions carefully. Insecticides are both plant- and pest-specific and so should be used only on the plants and pests listed on the label. There is no such thing as an all-purpose insecticide. If your plant or pest problem is not included on the label, the product is not intended to treat it.

In addition, adhere to the general guidelines below:

✳ Always use insecticides outside or in the garage with the door open. It is not wise to use insecticides in the house, where they will linger in the air. Avoid inhaling fumes or dust from any insecticides, even organics. Wear a face mask and goggles when using powders.

✳ Insecticides labeled "organic," or "natural," are dangerous nonetheless. Take all of the same precautions with organic insecticides that you would take with synthetics.

✳ Apply insecticides out of direct sunlight. Many insecticides begin to break down when exposed to light, thereby losing their effectiveness. This is especially true of organics.

✳ Be sure the soil is moist before you apply the insecticide. Otherwise the plant will not be able to absorb it.

Whether you decide to use an organic or synthetic insecticide, carefully follow the directions on the package for use, storage, and disposal. Repeated doses are usually necessary to eliminate all insects, so you will need to keep the products on hand. Be sure they're stored safely—in locked cabinets—out of the reach of children and pets.

Plant Diseases

Fortunately, houseplants that are well cared for rarely develop diseases. Houseplant diseases are mainly caused by bacteria and fungi. Bacteria-caused diseases tend to be more of a problem in greenhouses than in the average home. As a matter of fact, most plant bacteria are actually beneficial, helping plants absorb nutrients from the soil.

Fungi, on the other hand, are fairly common problems for houseplants. Like bacteria, fungi enter a plant through a wound or natural opening or by forcing their way into a plant's stems, leaves, or flowers.

FUNGAL DISEASES
Fungal spores are carried by wind, water, air, and tools. Fungi multiply rapidly in damp, low-lit conditions. In fact, moisture and low light are essential to their reproduction. Plants and soil

Disease or not? Spots on the geranium leaf (top) and begonia leaf (bottom) are not symptoms of disease. Possible causes are too much heat, direct sun, or fertilizer burn.

that remain too wet for too long invite fungal problems. Follow the watering instructions in the plant profiles beginning on page 108.

Botrytis and other fungal diseases once constantly plagued houseplants, but not any longer, because many plants today are bred to be disease resistant. Such diseases usually occur in a greenhouse or garden room full of plants, where the humidity might be too high or where conditions are otherwise favorable for diseases to take hold. Spots, rusts, mildew, and streaks on leaves are some signs that diseases are at work. Soft roots, wilts, and rots are other symptoms.

Botrytis Blight. If a gray, moldy growth starts to cover the leaves, stems, or flowers of a plant, botrytis blight may be the cause. This disease thrives on plants that have been overfed, overwatered, or overcrowded. Start by cutting off the affected leaves or stems. Decrease the water, and stop fertilizing. Divide the plant, or trim off some shoots to give it more room. If the outdoor temperature is not bitterly cold, open a window. Or install a fan near the plant to circulate the air.

Powdery Mildew. White, fuzzy growth that later turns brown is a sign of powdery mildew. Cut out all of the affected parts, and improve air circulation, as mentioned above.

Also, powdery mildew can be treated with a solution of baking soda and water, just as outdoor gardeners treat roses affected by powdery mildew. Mix 1 tablespoonful of baking soda and 1 tablespoonful of horticultural oil in 1 gallon of water. The oil helps the baking soda stick to the leaves. Spray the affected plant completely, paying special attention to the undersides of leaves.

If you remove plant parts damaged by disease or otherwise work around infected plants, wash your hands. Don't forget to sterilize your tools so you don't spread diseases from one plant to another.

PREVENTIVE MEASURES
The best defenses against plant diseases are a clean environment, proper growing conditions, and fresh air.

Try using horticultural charcoal to deter fungal disease, mildew, and many bacterial diseases on your houseplants. Highly effective, horticultural charcoal can be purchased in tidy sacks at nurseries, or you can simply use ashes from your fireplace. Just sprinkle the charcoal or ash onto the leaves of affected plants.

Note: As with plants that are heavily infested with insects, it may be wiser and less costly in the long run to discard a diseased plant and replace it.

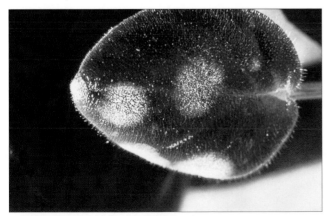

Powdery mildew on African violet (above) is caused by poor air circulation. Cut the leaf off at the base of its stem. Then improve air circulation around the plant.

This plant is not diseased. Insufficient water or too much fertilizer has burned it. Cut off the damaged leaves, water the plant thoroughly, and mist.

part Two

Plant Profiles

How to Read
  the Plant Profiles   107

Major Families   108

Other Families   176

part
Two

Plant Profiles

*T*he houseplants described in this second part of the book are widely available. Here you'll find traditional houseplants, such as Boston fern and philodendron, as well as a host of comparative newcomers. If you'd like to purchase any of these plants but don't find them at your retailer, inquire about ordering them.

The author has personally grown all plants described in this book. He directed the photography of most plants in this section as well as the step-by-step photos in the first part of this book. He decided not to include some plants often regarded as houseplants, such as agaves and pileas, because they didn't perform well indoors.—*The Editors*

THE FAMILY ARRANGEMENT

Plants profiled on the upcoming pages are arranged within two subsections. Each subsection groups the plants alphabetically by the family common name, such as Begonias, Cacti, and Ferns. Within each family, the plants are arranged alphabetically by the scientific name for the genus and species. The first subsection, beginning on page 108, covers the major families— those that include the vast majority of houseplants. The second subsection, beginning on page 176, features excellent houseplants from families that contain a much smaller portion of readily available houseplants.

Yet there's a more practical reason for the two sub-sections. It allows the grouping of plants from major families on whole pages and two-page "spreads," thereby helping you see the similarities and differences within families and genera (plural for genus).

THE PROFILES

Each profile includes the kinds of information shown on the next page. Here's more on growing factors:

Light. Although all growing factors mentioned below work together, light should be your first consideration in placing a plant. See also pages 58–61.

Soil. Most plants grow well in all-purpose potting soil. Packaged houseplant soil generally contains all the nutrients plants need. Yet some plants prefer a richer soil, which you can supply by adding sterile humus (compost) to your potting soil. Also, many cacti and succulents like a mix of potting soil and sand. Bromeliads and orchids grow better when planted in fir bark. See also pages 64–65.

Temperature & Humidity. Most plants adjust to average household temperatures of 70°F or higher with a drop of about 10°F at night. Exceptions are noted in individual profiles. See also pages 69–70.

Water. Soil kept evenly moist usually works best. Some plants like a little less water in winter and when resting, such as after blooming. You'll find these preferences noted. See also pages 68 and 74–77.

Fertilizer. Most of the profiles include a recommended fertilizer ratio for Nitrogen (N), Phosphorus (P), and Potassium (K), expressed in that sequence on packaging as percentages of the entire mix, thus: 20-10-10 or 10-10-10 for general-purpose fertilizer.

How to Read the Plant Profiles

Aroids (ARACEAE)

Family common name

Family scientific (botanical) name (See the family descriptions in Chapter 1, beginning on page 11, and Aroids specifically on pages 116–127.)

Common name used by most plant sellers

Scientific (botanical) name The first word is the *genus*, which usually contains a collection of similar species. The "×" symbol means that this plant is a hybrid, resulting from crossbreeding of different plants. The species name follows the genus. The genus and species names are conventionally shown in italic. For detailed definitions of these terms, see the "Glossary," pages 186–187.

Light needs

Soil and water needs

Temperature needs

Fertilizer needs

Cultivar is short for *cultivated variety* (not found in nature) and is expressed within single quotation marks.

The photograph may show a mature plant or an immature plant that looks more like young plants you'll find at retailers. When immature plants are shown, consult the text for a description of the full-grown plant.

aka is short for "also known as." Scientific nomenclature changes as research reveals new plant relationships. Thus older references and some retailers may list this plant as *Caladium bicolor*. In this case, the "C" is the abbreviation for *Caladium*, referring to its mention in preceding text.

Fancy-leaved Caladium
Caladium × hortulanum
(aka *C. bicolor* and other botanical names)

- Medium size
- Likes moderate light
- Easy to grow

Fancy-leaved caladiums are showy <u>foliage plants</u> with heart-shaped leaves in different combinations of red, pink, white, with various shades of green. There are hundreds of hybrids. Caladiums are grown from frost-tender tubers. Caladiums thrive in moderate light. Grow in an all-purpose potting soil kept quite moist during the growing season. The plants prefer warmth, with nighttime temperatures of at least 65°F. Feed with 10-10-10 ferilizer every two months during the growing season but not at all when dormant (mostly in winter). Start new plants from tubers.

Good cultivars: 'Pink Beauty', 'Rosebud', 'Frieda Hemple'

At-a-glance highlights include probable maximum heights, as follows:

Small: to 18 inches
Medium size: to 36 inches
Large: 36 inches & taller

Meaning that these plants are grown mainly for their foliage. Many foliage plants will bear flowers under favorable conditions.

Propagation method (See Chapter 6 for step-by-step photos and captions, and see page 91 for propagation from bulbs, corms, and tubers.)

PLANT PROFILES

Acanthus Family (ACANTHACEAE)

Zebra Plant, Yellow Plume Plant

Aphelandra squarrosa

- ❧ **Cheerful yellow flowers**
- ❧ **Handsome foliage**
- ❧ **Good small to medium-size plant**

From South American tropical forests, this plant has green leaves ribbed in white that provide a dramatic contrast. The plant grows upright to 24 inches and can get leggy. A plume of yellow flowers with bright yellow bracts appears at the top, usually in summer.

Yellow plume plant appreciates a bright location and grows well in standard all-purpose houseplant soil. Keep the soil evenly moist except in midwinter, when a month-long rest is needed. Keep the soil only barely moist at this time. Feed monthly with 20-10-10 plant food (except during the midwinter rest), and repot yearly in fresh soil. Prune when the plant gets too leggy. Propagate new plants from cuttings.

Firecracker Flower

Crossandra infundibuliformis

- ❧ **Popular medium-size houseplant**
- ❧ **Desirable orange flowers**
- ❧ **Requires careful cultivation**

In its native environment in India and southeastern Asia, firecracker flower can grow into a large bush. As a houseplant, though, it rarely grows taller than 30 inches. The attractive orange flowers pop out one after the other; hence, the common name. In spring, the flowers make this a decorative plant that is worth the necessary careful cultivation.

Grow firecracker flower in a bright window. Use a small pot of standard all-purpose houseplant soil. This plant requires precise watering and feeding, so keep the soil evenly moist. Feed monthly with 20-20-10 fertilizer, and repot in fresh soil every second year. Start new plants from stem cuttings.

Mosaic Plant
Fittonia verschaffeltii

- **Pretty veined foliage**
- **Excellent small windowsill plant**
- **Tolerates moderate to low light**

This subtly beautiful Peruvian native deserves greater recognition. Compact, it grows to about 24 inches and makes a handsome display in a hanging basket. The name mosaic alludes to the fine reticulation, or network of veins, in the foliage—pink to reddish veins crisscross the deep green leaves in a netlike pattern.

Grow mosaic plant in standard all-purpose houseplant soil kept evenly moist all year. Use a small pot because the plant grows best when potbound. Repot when roots extend from the drainage holes. Feed monthly with 10-10-10 fertilizer. Propagate new plants from cuttings.

Polka Dot Plant
Hypoestes phyllostachya (aka *H. sanguinolenta*)

- **Small and attractive**
- **Good window plant**
- **Colorful foliage**

A fast-growing plant from Madagascar, polka dot plant is a good choice for a bright windowsill. For greater visual impact, put two plants in one container. The common name, "polka dot," derives from the pink spots sprinkled over the foliage.

Grow this plant in standard all-purpose houseplant soil, and allow the soil to dry out between waterings. The plant tends to get leggy, so cut back the stems to encourage a bushier, more compact form. Feed monthly with 10-10-10 fertilizer. Start new plants from cuttings.

Acanthus Family cont'd

Shrimp Plant

Justicia brandegeana (aka Beloperone guttata)

* **Long-time favorite**
* **Medium size**
* **Easy to grow**

The shrimp plant bears curved, shrimp-like spikes of pinkish or yellow bracts for most of the year. This plant is bushy and can grow as tall as 36 inches if left unpruned. It makes a good window plant.

To develop the best color, provide a bright location with some direct sun. Use standard all-purpose houseplant soil, and keep it evenly moist, except in winter when watering can be decreased somewhat. Feed monthly with 20-10-10 fertilizer. Shrimp plant becomes leggy if you don't prune as needed; cut back the stems to keep the plant compact and bushy. Repot annually in fresh soil. Propagate new plants from stem cuttings.

Lollipop Plant, Yellow Shrimp Plant

Pachystachys lutea

* **Fine yellow flower spikes**
* **Good small table plant**
* **Needs little care**

From Peru, this plant has a history of changes in its botanic name. It was first introduced as *Beloperone*. Later it was called *Justicia*, and now it is known as *Pachystachys*. In any case, it somewhat resembles the shrimp plant, above, except that the plumes stand straight up and are bright yellow. The flower spikes consist of tiny white flowers peeking out from overlapping yellow bracts.

Grow yellow shrimp plant in bright but indirect light, in standard all-purpose houseplant soil. But make sure the soil drains readily. Keep the soil evenly moist all year, and feed monthly with 10-10-10 fertilizer. Prune the stems when the plant gets leggy. Propagate new plants from stem cuttings.

SANCHEZIA SPECIOSA
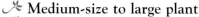
Sanchezia speciosa (aka *S. nobilis*)

- **Medium-size to large plant**
- **Fine attractive leaves**
- **Easy to grow**

Warm-climate gardeners know sanchezia as an outdoor plant, but it grows well indoors, too. A pretty and undemanding foliage plant from Ecuador, sanchezia has green leaves with prominent yellow veins. It is shrubby in form but can be kept in bounds with light pruning.

Grow sanchezia in bright light in all-purpose potting soil. Keep the soil evenly moist all year, and mist the leaves regularly—this plant likes moisture and high humidity. Feed monthly with 10-10-10 fertilizer. Propagate new plants from stem cuttings.

PERSIAN SHIELD PLANT
Strobilanthes dyerianus

- **Stunning foliage**
- **Medium-size, compact grower**
- **Great room accent**

This lovely foliage plant has fine-toothed leaves in a unique purple-green combination that commands attention. Pale blue flowers occasionally appear, but, this plant is usually grown for its striking foliage. Persian shield plant looks great on any desk or table. The plant grows vertically to 30 inches.

Grow Persian shield plant in a temperate location in bright but indirect light. Use a standard all-purpose houseplant soil kept evenly moist in warm months and somewhat drier in cool months.

Do not mist the leaves. Feed quarterly with 10-10-10 fertilizer. If the plant gets straggly, cut it back somewhat. Repot only when the plant is potbound, usually about every second year. Propagate new plants from stem cuttings.

Amaryllis Family (AMARYLLIDACEAE)

Kaffir Lily
Clivia miniata

- **Dependable spring bloomer**
- **Striking flowers**
- **Medium size**

In spring, Kaffir lily produces a cluster of vivid orange, trumpet-shaped flowers with yellow centers above strap-shaped, glossy, deep green leaves.

This plant prefers to be out of direct sun and tolerates low light. It thrives in cool temperatures. Grow in a large pot of rich, humusy soil, and keep the soil evenly moist all year. Kaffir lily likes to be potbound and can be grown in the same pot for many years. Instead of repotting, topdress with 4 inches of new soil every year. Feed quarterly with 20-10-10 fertilizer. Propagate new plants by division.

Amazon Lily
Eucharis × grandiflora

- **Medium size**
- **Lovely fragrant white flowers**
- **Easy to grow**

Amazon lily bears fragrant white, star-shaped, lily-like flowers on erect stems. The leaves of this 30-inch plant are large and glossy dark green.

Grow Amazon lily in a somewhat sunny space with moderate temperatures in rich, humusy soil. Use a small container because the plant does best when potbound. Keep the soil evenly moist until the plant finishes blooming. Let the bulb dry out for a month or so; then start routine watering again. The plant may rebloom in a few months. Fertilize with 10-20-10 plant food every month, except when the plant is resting just after it finishes blooming. Propagate new plants by division. See Chapter 6, page 91, for tips on growing bulbs indoors.

FIREBALL, CATHERINE WHEEL

Haemanthus katherinae (aka Scadoxus multiflorus ssp. katherinae)

- ✂ **Fine cut flowers**
- ✂ **Stunning bright red blooms**
- ✂ **Small, easy to grow**

This bulbous plant from South Africa produces a sphere of small starlike red flowers on an erect stem. The bulb can be started at almost any time of year. Flowers bloom about nine months later.

This plant likes bright light and average household temperatures. Grow in a 6- to 8-inch pot, and leave the tip of the bulb exposed above the soil line. Use a rich soil; add extra humus to the all-purpose potting soil described in Chapter 5, on page 64. Water fireball moderately, and increase watering as the stem grows so that the soil stays evenly moist. Feed once or twice monthly with 10-10-10 fertilizer. After flowering, stop watering the bulb to allow the plant to rest. After about six months, repot in fresh soil so it blooms again. Fireball is difficult to propagate at home; to start new plants, buy new bulbs.

AMARYLLIS

Hippeastrum cultivars

- ✂ **Gift plant**
- ✂ **Medium size, with huge flowers**
- ✂ **Easy to grow**

The original species from South America has given rise to dozens of cultivars: red, pink, orange, salmon, white, and streaked. The flowers—some 7 inches across—bloom just a few months after bulb planting.

Plant the bulb with the top half above the soil line in a pot just large enough to hold it. Grow in a bright location with some direct sun, in all-purpose potting mix. Water sparingly at first; then keep the soil evenly moist when growth appears. After flowering, cut off the thick flower stalk, and let the leaves grow for a few months to nourish the bulb. Gradually reduce watering so that the leaves turn brown and die back. Stop watering, remove the dead leaves, and give the plant a dry rest. Store the bulb in a paper bag in a dark, dry place. In two months plant it again in fresh soil. There's no need to feed the plant because the bulb nourishes the flowers. Start new plants from offsets, or purchase new bulbs.

Aralia Family (ARALIACEAE)

🌿 FINGER ARALIA, FALSE ARALIA
Dizygotheca elegantissima (aka *Schefflera elegantissima*)

- 🌿 Graceful large plant
- 🌿 Good vertical plant
- 🌿 Easy to grow

This Pacific Island native is welcome in the indoor garden for its lacy, airy grace. It can grow to 48 inches high. The slender leaflets, arranged in a circle around the tops of the stems, look rather like fingers; hence the common name. This plant is easy to grow if given good routine care, but it cannot withstand neglect.

Supply bright light and sustained moisture at the roots. Grow aralia in standard all-purpose houseplant soil, and provide good drainage. Feed monthly with 10-10-10 fertilizer. Propagate from cuttings.

🌿 ENGLISH IVY
Hedera helix

- 🌿 One of the best trailing plants
- 🌿 Many hybrids available
- 🌿 Fresh green beauty

With its lobed leaves and lush growth, English Ivy has been a household tradition. Today there are countless hybrids, some with plain green leaves, others with foliage variegated with yellow or creamy white. Ivies make good room accents.

Provide bright light and well-drained all-purpose soil that is kept evenly moist but never soggy. Feed quarterly with 20-10-10 fertilizer. Propagate new plants from leaf or stem cuttings.

Good cultivars: 'Gold Dust', 'Glacier', 'Curlilocks'

🌿 MING ARALIA
Polyscias fruticosa

- 🌿 Pretty, medium-size foliage plant
- 🌿 Heart-shaped leaves
- 🌿 Slow grower

A pretty but not sensational plant from Polynesia, ming aralia grows 24 to 30 inches, with attractive crinkled foliage. Decorative, it is easy to grow indoors. Try it if you have space.

Grow ming aralia in a bright location, in a small pot of standard all-purpose houseplant soil. Keep the soil evenly moist. Feed monthly with 10-10-10 fertilizer. Maintain warm temperatures because ming aralia does not tolerate cold well. Propagate new plants from cuttings.

ꞵALFOUR ARALIA
Polyscias scutellaria 'Balfourii' (aka *P. balfouriana*)

- ✺ **A handsome, tall vertical plant**
- ✺ **Small round leaves**
- ✺ **Good foliage plant**

This vertical plant grows to 48 inches. It has a central stem and frilly small round leaves. There are several varieties, some with variegated foliage. Most make handsome room plants.

Grow Balfour aralia in a warm bright location in standard all-purpose houseplant soil. Water and then allow the soil to dry out before watering again. Feed quarterly with 20-20-20 fertilizer. Propagate new plants from tip cuttings.

Good cultivars: 'Marginata', 'Pennockii'

𝒱ARIEGATED UMBRELLA PLANT
Schefflera actinophylla 'Variegata'

- ✺ **Handsome variegated leaves**
- ✺ **Large plant**
- ✺ **Easy to grow**

This popular plant is a good addition to the indoor garden. Its oblong leaflets are graceful looking, and the plant brings a hint of the tropics into a home. Its branching habit and shiny green leaves edged with white distinguish it from the typical green scheffleras. It tolerates a range of conditions and makes a good room accent. *Schefflera* is sometimes listed by the genus name *Brassaia*.

Grow umbrella plant in bright light with no direct sun. Pot it in standard all-purpose houseplant soil, and keep the soil evenly moist. Feed quarterly with 20-10-10 fertilizer. (See young plants in various stages of development on page 82.) If the plant gets too leggy, cut the lower stems. Propagate new plants from cuttings.

Aroids (ARACEAE)

Amelia Chinese Evergreen
Aglaonema 'Amelia'

- Handsome foliage
- Medium size
- Easy to grow

Attractive green foliage mottled with lighter gray-green sets 'Amelia' apart. This elegant plant grows to 30 inches and can take neglect.

Grow 'Amelia' in bright light but not direct sun, in all-purpose, well-draining houseplant soil. Keep the soil evenly moist all year. Feed monthly with 20-10-10 fertilizer. 'Amelia' tolerates temperatures as low as 55° to 60°F at night. Propagate by division.

Camilla Chinese Evergreen
Aglaonema 'Camilla'

- Tolerates neglect
- Medium size
- Easy to grow

Both beautiful and durable, 'Camilla' is variable in leaf color. This Southeast Asian native was introduced in 1856 and grows to about 30 inches.

Grow the plant in bright light but not direct sun, and use a standard all-purpose potting soil. Keep the soil evenly moist, and feed twice a month with 20-10-5 plant food. Repot annually. Propagate new plants from stem cuttings.

Other good cultivars: 'Silver Queen', 'Silver Spear'

Shield Plant
Alocasia × *amazonica*

- Exotic appearance
- Medium size
- Dislikes nighttime temperatures below 55°F

From tropical Asia, this dramatic plant offers showy green velvety foliage with contrasting copper, gray, silver, or red veins. Large arrow-head-shaped leaves float atop tall stems. The plants may go dormant if chilled or allowed to dry out but after a few months will resume growth.

Provide bright light (but not direct sun) and warm temperatures. Add a little peat moss to the potting mix, and keep it evenly moist. Feed once a month with 20-10-10 fertilizer. Repot annually. Propagate by division.

BLACK VELVET ALOCASIA
Alocasia 'Black Velvet'

- **Small to medium-size plant**
- **Dramatic foliage**
- **Survives cool temperatures**

This robust hybrid of Asian heritage grows to 24 inches. The leaves, on short stems, have a striking greenish black sheen.

Grow 'Black Velvet' in all-purpose potting soil kept evenly moist (but not soggy) all year. Do not overwater. Avoid getting water on leaves; otherwise they will spot. The plant can withstand some coolness, but nighttime temperatures should never drop below 50°F. Repot every second year. Feed monthly with 20-10-10 plant food. Propagate new plants by division.

COPPER ALOCASIA
Alocasia cuprea

- **Small to medium-size plant**
- **Attractive foliage**
- **Survives cool temperatures**

The arrowhead-shaped leaves of this native of Borneo are an outstanding burnished copper color. This alocasia grows slowly to 20 inches tall and is a good plant for a desk or table.

A low-light northern-window exposure is ideal for this plant. Grow copper alocasia in a mix of equal parts fine-grade fir bark and all-purpose houseplant soil. Keep the soil evenly moist, never too dry or too wet; otherwise the leaves become limp. Feed once a month with 10-10-10 fertilizer. Copper alocasia will withstand temperatures to about 55°F, and that's lower than most alocasias can handle. Propagate new plants by division.

Aroids cont'd

Green Goddess Alocasia

Alocasia 'Green Goddess'

- ❧ **Medium size to tall**
- ❧ **Likes low light**
- ❧ **Exquisite heart-shaped leaves mottled with light green and dark green**

With large heart-shaped leaves on tall graceful stems, 'Green Goddess' is an exotic plant that grows to 36 inches. The rich green foliage shaded with green-black commands attention.

Grow the plant in a somewhat low-light location with temperatures above 60°F. Keep the plant out of drafts, which cause the leaves to fold. Use a humusy soil that drains well; add extra humus to all-purpose potting soil as described in Chapter 5, page 64. Keep the soil evenly moist all year except in winter, when the soil can be allowed to go somewhat dry. Feed only in spring and summer with 20-20-20 plant food. Propagate by division.

Tailflower

Anthurium hookeri

- ❧ **Medium size**
- ❧ **Fountainlike form**
- ❧ **Grown for foliage**

This species, from the West Indies, has large heart-shaped leaves in a fountain or rosette form. Although seldom encountered in retail stores, it is available if you make enough inquiries. It makes a worthwhile edition to the indoor garden. A compact plant, it grows to about 30 inches in diameter.

Tailflower likes a low-light location, such as a north window, and good air circulation. Grow the plant in a mix of equal parts fine-grade fir bark and potting soil kept evenly moist all year. Good drainage is essential; otherwise the plant can develop root rot. Feed quarterly with 20-10-10 fertilizer. Propagate new plants by division.

*F*LAMINGO FLOWER

Anthurium scherzerianum and *A. andraeanum*

- **Medium size**
- **Long-lasting flowers**
- **Excellent cut flower**

The flowering spathes of flamingo flower can last an astounding six weeks. Many hybrids are available, with flowers in a variety of warm colors. Originally from Costa Rica, the plant is now widely grown in Hawaii. It is the most popular houseplant in the genus.

Grow flamingo flower in bright light in an all-purpose potting soil. Keep the soil evenly moist. Provide good ventilation, and feed monthly with a 20-20-10 fertilizer. Repot annually. Grow new plants by division.

Good cultivars: 'Southern Blush' and 'Lady Jane'

*F*ANCY-LEAVED CALADIUM

Caladium × hortulanum
(aka *C. bicolor*)

- **Medium size**
- **Likes moderate light**
- **Easy to grow**

Native to Brazil, fancy-leaved caladiums are showy foliage plants with heart-shaped leaves in different combinations of red, pink, white, with various shades of green. There are hundreds of hybrids. Caladiums are grown from frost-tender tubers.

Caladiums thrive in moderate light and grow in an all-purpose potting soil kept quite moist during the growing season. The plants prefer warmth, with nighttime temperatures of at least 65°F. Feed with 10-10-10 ferilizer every two months during the growing season, but not at all when dormant (mostly in winter). Start new plants from tubers.

Good cultivars: 'Pink Beauty', 'Rosebud', 'Frieda Hemple'

$\mathcal{A}$roids cont'd

$\mathcal{H}$ILO BEAUTY COLOCASIA

Colocasia 'Hilo Beauty' (aka *Alocasia* 'Hilo Beauty')

- ❧ **Compact growth, medium size**
- ❧ **Colorful foliage**
- ❧ **Highly recommended**

The colocasias are sometimes considered inappropriate for the indoors because of their large leaves and sprawling growth habit. However, 'Hilo Beauty', a recent hybrid, has smaller leaves mottled green and yellow, and its slow, compact growth—to about 24 inches—makes it more suitable for most homes.

Grow 'Hilo Beauty' in standard all-purpose houseplant soil kept evenly moist all year. Place it in a bright but not sunny location, and feed quarterly with 10-20-10 fertilizer. This is an outstanding foliage plant because the leaves are borne on erect stems and create a beautiful picture. Propagate this plant by division.

$\mathcal{C}$AMILLE DUMBCANE

Dieffenbachia picta 'Camille'

- ❧ **Large plant**
- ❧ **Colorful foliage**
- ❧ **Many available cultivars**

Dumbcane is native to the tropical Americas. Characterized by splashed, speckled, and splotched foliage—white on green, yellow and green, shades of green—this dieffenbachia offers bright, vibrant, colorful leaves in a host of variegation patterns. All parts of the plant are poisonous and cause the mouth and tongue to swell if chewed; hence the common name. Keep it away from small children and pets.

Grow dieffenbachia in bright light with an all-purpose potting soil that drains readily. Feed monthly with 20-20-10 plant food, and keep plants in a warm location away from drafts. Repot in fresh soil every second year. Start new plants from cuttings.

Other good cultivars: 'Tropic Snow'; 'Exotica' and its variants

Exotica Dumbcane
Dieffenbachia picta 'Exotica'

- **Medium plant**
- **Handsome patterned leaves**
- **Easy to grow**

With handsome broad leaves splotched yellow and green, 'Exotica' grows to about 30 inches tall from a central trunk. This excellent, compact plant can tolerate neglect.

'Exotica' likes an evenly moist, standard all-purpose houseplant soil. Put the plant in a bright but not sunny location, and feed it monthly with 10-20-10 fertilizer. Propagate by air layering.

Tropic Snow Dumbcane
Dieffenbachia 'Tropic Snow'

- **Medium size**
- **Handsome foliage**
- **Easy to grow**

With broad leaves patterned in green and white, this dieffenbachia is attractive and popular. It is compact, rarely growing more than 36 inches.

Plant 'Tropic Snow' in standard houseplant soil, and keep it evenly moist all year. Place it in a bright but not sunny area, and feed with 20-20-20 plant food every fourth month. Wipe leaves occasionally with a damp cloth. Propagate by air layering.

Marble Queen Pothos
Epipremnum aureum 'Marble Queen' (aka *Scindapsus* and *Philodendron*)

- **Good vining plant**
- **Bushy appearance**
- **Grows fast**

With green heart-shaped leaves handsomely splashed with white on long trailing stems, this pothos cultivar either climbs or trails. Support the stems on a piece of bark or a trellis inserted into the soil, or grow the plant in a hanging basket. Pothos tolerates almost any indoor conditions, but for optimal growth give it bright light, and keep the soil evenly moist. Trim back overlong stems, and feed twice a month with 20-10-10 fertilizer. New plants root easily from cuttings.

Other good cultivars: 'Wilcoxii', 'Golden Pothos'

Aroids cont'd

Satin Pothos

Epipremnum 'Satin'

- **Vining plant**
- **Handsome foliage**
- **Easy to grow**

Referred to as an epipremnum (its scientific name) or a pothos (its common name), 'Satin' is a new introduction. Offering beautiful, satiny gray-green heart-shaped leaves, it grows slowly to 24 inches and is compact in habit.

Grow 'Satin' in a bright location. Plant it in a standard all-purpose houseplant soil, and be sure drainage is good. This plant does not tolerate over-watering. Feed quarterly with 20-10-10 plant food. A fine new edition to the pothos family, sure to become a traditional favorite, 'Satin' grows best in a small pot. Propagate from tip cuttings.

Emerald Gem Homalomena

Homalomena rubescens 'Emerald Gem'

- **Small to medium size**
- **Lush decorative plant**
- **Handsome foliage**

The parent species of this handsome aroid cultivar with heart-shaped, dark green leaves is native to Java. 'Emerald Gem' tends to grow in the shape of a compact bouquet. This is a lush foliage plant that has been overlooked and has only recently become widely available. The heart-shaped leaves are especially desirable, and the plant stays compact.

Grow 'Emerald Gem' in dappled sunlight, in a rich potting soil kept evenly moist. Feed quarterly with 20-10-10 fertilizer. Wipe the leaves occasionally with a damp cloth to keep them clean. Repot infrequently; the plant dislikes having its roots disturbed. Propagate by division.

SWISS CHEESE PLANT
Monstera deliciosa

- ✤ **Very large when mature**
- ✤ **Ideal for large tubs**
- ✤ **Generally easy to grow**

When young, this plant has smooth leaves. But as it matures and the leaves grow larger, the leaves develop deeply cut edges and wide holes, inspiring the nickname, Swiss cheese plant. The slashes, holes, or cuts in the huge leaves enable them to withstand strong winds and heavy rains in their native Central American jungles. Mature plants can reach 8 or more feet in height, with leaves up to 18 inches long.

Grow this plant in a bright but not sunny location. Provide a large tub of standard all-purpose houseplant soil that drains well, and give the plant plenty of water. Use a trellis for added support. Feed monthly with a 10-10-10 fertilizer. Keep the plant away from drafts, and wipe the leaves with a damp cloth occasionally. Topdress with fresh soil once a year, and repot the plant only when it is potbound. Propagate from stem cuttings or by air layering.

Good cultivars: 'Albovariegata' and 'Laceleaf'

NEPHTHYTIS
Nephthytis hybrid

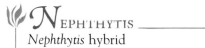

- ✤ **Small plant**
- ✤ **Handsome bronze foliage**
- ✤ **Easy to grow**

Striking broad, bronze foliage is the main asset of nephthytis, which is sometimes included in the genus *Syngonium*. But nephthytis is only a distant cousin to the plants in that genus, and there is little family resemblance.

Give nephthytis a bright but not sunny location, and pot it in standard houseplant soil. Keep the soil evenly moist, and fertilize with 10-20-20 every month. Propagate by division.

Aroids cont'd

Philodendron
Philodendron squamiferum

- Medium size
- Fine bushy philodendron
- Handsome hanging plant

This attractive philodendron, with handsome lobed green leaves and fuzzy stems, is a slow grower that needs little attention.

Grow the plant in a bright but not sunny location. Plant it in a standard all-purpose houseplant soil. Let the soil dry out between waterings; the plant dislikes soggy conditions. Wipe leaves with a damp cloth occasionally to best display the glossy green foliage. Feed monthly with 10-10-10 fertilizer. Propagate by division.

Xanadu Philodendron
Philodendron 'Xanadu'

- Medium size
- Needs minimal care
- Slow growing

'Xanadu' is a recent introduction. Unlike the familiar trailing philodendrons, this handsome cultivar grows upright, to 30 inches tall, with shiny green lance-shaped leaves. It eventually resembles a bouquet of leaves.

Give this low-maintenance plant bright light without direct sun, and grow it in a standard all-purpose houseplant soil. Keep the soil evenly moist all year. Feed monthly with 20-10-10 fertilizer. Start new plants by division.

Domino Peace Lily
Spathiphyllum 'Domino'

- ❧ **Medium size**
- ❧ **Attractive foliage**
- ❧ **Fine vertical growth habit**

This beautiful new spathiphyllum cultivar has attractively mottled white-and-green lance-shaped leaves. 'Domino' grows to about 30 inches tall and achieves an elegant upright appearance.

To maintain the foliage variegation (contrasting colors within the leaves), this cultivar needs more light than the plain-leaved species. So grow this plant in bright light but not direct sun. Use standard all-purpose houseplant soil kept evenly moist except in winter, when the plant can be allowed to dry out somewhat. Feed quarterly with 20-10-10 fertilizer. Propagate by division.

White-flag Plant
Spathiphyllum floribundum

- ❧ **Large plant**
- ❧ **Rarely attacked by pests**
- ❧ **Easy to grow**

Spathiphyllums offer white flowers, consisting of a slender spadix surrounded by a hoodlike spathe, somewhat similar in structure to those of their aroid cousins, the anthuriums. From Colombia and South America, spathiphyllum species include several undemanding, adaptable houseplants that grow to 38 inches. They tolerate low levels of light. There are many cultivars to choose from.

Spathiphyllums prefer a bright location without direct sun. Plant them in standard all-purpose potting soil kept evenly moist except in winter, when it can be allowed to dry out somewhat between waterings. *Note:* This plant will not flower if it is not kept moist. Topdress yearly with fresh soil, and feed plants once a month with 20-20-10 fertilizer. Propagate by root division.

Good cultivars: 'Marion Wagne' and 'Mauna Loa'

$\mathscr{A}$roids cont'd

$\mathscr{A}$rrowhead Plant
Syngonium podophyllum

- Medium-size climber
- Elegant
- Easy to grow

The tropical syngoniums (sometimes called neph-thytis) are attractive, generally smallish plants that are bushy but vining. There are many hybrids offering colorful foliage.

Arrowhead plant is fast growing and easy to cultivate. It prefers bright light without direct sun but will adapt to lower light. Give it well-drained soil kept evenly moist all year. Feed once a month with 10-10-10 fertilizer. Support the climbing stems with a small trellis in the pot, or grow the plant in a hanging basket. Grow new plants from cuttings.

Good cultivars: 'Emerald Gem', 'Imperial White', 'Frosted Valentine'

$\mathscr{A}$ngel's Wings
Xanthosoma lindenii (aka *Caladium lindenii*)

- Medium size
- Decorative white-marked leaves
- Easy to grow

This plant from Central America has attractive large white-veined leaves and grows to about 30 inches. Seldom encountered at retail stores, this plant deserves more attention. If you don't find it at your plant store, you can inquire about ordering it.

Xanthosoma does best in a bright but not sunny location. Give it a small pot of standard houseplant soil kept evenly moist all year. Feed this plant monthly with 10-10-10 fertilizer. Propagate by division.

GOLDEN CALLA LILY
Zantedeschia elliottiana

- **Small to medium size**
- **Pretty, colorful flowers**
- **Easy to grow**

Most small calla lily cultivars available today grow to 20 inches and have large oblong leaves and splendid short-stemmed flowers consisting of a slender spadix surrounded by a smooth hood-like spathe. Calla lilies grow from bulblike structures called rhizomes and are easily started almost any time of year. They are generally available around Easter. Many flowers are produced on each plant.

Keep this calla in a bright, somewhat sunny location while it is growing. Wet the soil until water drains from the bottom of the pot. It's time to water when the soil is dry an inch down. Use a rich soil, but there's no need to fertilize. After blooming, rest it for three months; then repot rhizomes in fresh soil.

PINK CALLA LILY
Zantedeschia rehmannii

- **Small to medium**
- **Lovely pink flowers**
- **Easy to grow**

This charming plant from South Africa has handsome green leaves and pretty pink flowers with the classic calla lily form. Other color forms are available in pastel shades as well as classic white. The plant is easily grown from a rhizome and is now available in supermarkets at holidays.

Grow the pink calla in a bright location, in humusy soil that drains readily. Keep the soil evenly moist. Plant rhizomes any time you find them for sale; flowers appear in 6 to 8 weeks. Do not feed the plant. Start new plants from rhizomes. See calla lily above.

Begonia Family (BEGONIACEAE)

Cleopatra Begonia
Begonia 'Cleopatra'

- **Large basket plant**
- **Stunning foliage**
- **Tolerates low light**

Handsome, colorful maple-shaped leaves make this begonia a favorite. It's also an excellent hanging plant, growing to 36 inches in diameter. Small pink flowers are borne in clusters in summer, but the foliage is the asset. Use this plant to brighten dim corners of rooms.

'Cleopatra' grows in moderate light. It likes standard all-purpose houseplant soil kept evenly moist all year. Trim back the stems occasionally to keep it compact. Feed monthly with 20-10-10 fertilizer. Propagate from leaf cuttings.

Reiger Begonia
Begonia × hiemalis

- **Medium size**
- **Many flowers**
- **Easy to grow**

Reiger begonias bear abundant blooms in a range of bright colors—yellow, red, and orange—akin to tuberous begonias. These compact, bushy plants grow from a corm (bulb) and reach 20 inches tall with dark green leaves. Reiger begonias are often sold as gift plants.

Give Reiger begonias a bright location with some sun. They need evenly moist all-purpose potting soil. Unless you provide thorough drainage, the plants will soon perish. Most Reiger begonias are used as temporary plants—expect them to last six months or so. But to keep them growing, repot in fresh soil annually. Feed semiannually with 10-20-10 fertilizer. Reigers are difficult to propagate, so purchase new plants from suppliers.

KEWENSIS BEGONIA
Begonia 'Kewensis'

- ❧ **Grows quickly to 40 inches**
- ❧ **Handsome dark green foliage**
- ❧ **Lovely hanging plant**

Striking angel-wing bronze foliage creates a dense-leaved halo of color around this choice hybrid. Small white flowers appear in spring and summer. The mature plant is stunning on a tabletop or trailing in a hanging basket.

Keep in bright light for maximum leaf color. Plant in standard all-purpose houseplant soil that's kept evenly moist. Feed monthly with 10-10-10 fertilizer. Propagate by division.

RED-LEAF BEGONIA
Begonia hybrid

- ❧ **Excellent medium-size hanging plant**
- ❧ **Lovely red foliage**
- ❧ **Easy to grow**

Rounded, red-hued leaves are this begonia's main asset. Plant in a hanging basket, and the somewhat pendant stems will trail attractively. Red-leaf begonia grows rapidly to 30 inches in diameter and requires little care.

Place Red-leaf begonia in a brightly lit location out of direct sun. Grow in standard all-purpose houseplant soil that drains readily. Keep the soil evenly moist all year. Red-leaf tolerates both cool and warm home temperatures. Feed quarterly with 10-10-10 fertilizer. Propagate by division.

WATERMELON BEGONIA
Pellionia repens (aka *Elatostema repens*)

- ❧ **Good creeper for terrariums**
- ❧ **Mottled foliage**
- ❧ **Grows in part shade**

Although called a begonia, this plant is actually in the Urticaceae family. These creeping plants grow to 4 inches high and are useful in hanging baskets or terrariums. The oval leaves, to 2½ inches long, are a mottled dark green, sometimes tinged with brownish purple.

Grow in moist, well-drained, loamy soil in indirect light. Needs humidity and warmth; keep away from drafts. Propagate by stem cuttings.

Begonia Family cont'd

 ## Angel-wing Begonia
Begonia hybrid

- Medium size
- Many flowers
- Handsome in baskets

The canelike stems of angel-wing begonias cascade gracefully from hanging baskets and grow to about 30 inches. The leaves are shaped like angel's wings and may be light or dark green, solidly colored, or spotted with white. During warm months, angel-wing begonias bear masses of small flowers.

Most angel-wings need a sunny location and plenty of water. They don't do well in drafts. Grow in all-purpose houseplant soil. Feed with 20-10-10 plant food. Maintain a vigil for insects. Propagate from leaf, stem, or tip cuttings.

Rex Begonia
Begonia Rex-Cultorum hybrid

- Compact habit, medium size
- Exquisite colorful foliage
- Moderate light

Sometimes called tapestry plants because of their exquisite foliage, rex begonia hybrids have been favorite houseplants for decades. There are now hundreds of hybrids. The wing-shaped foliage has irregularly notched or ruffled edges and is streaked, veined, and splashed with combinations of silver or various shades of green, pink, rose, red, maroon, purple, brown, or black. The plants grow to 24 inches.

Grow rex begonias in bright to moderate light in a rich soil. Keep the soil evenly moist, and fertilize twice a year with 10-10-10 plant food. Avoid getting water on leaves, or they will spot. Start new plants from leaf cuttings.

 ## Picotee Begonia
Begonia 'Picotee'

- Medium size
- Long-lasting flowers
- Many flowers

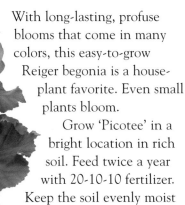

With long-lasting, profuse blooms that come in many colors, this easy-to-grow Reiger begonia is a houseplant favorite. Even small plants bloom.

Grow 'Picotee' in a bright location in rich soil. Feed twice a year with 20-10-10 fertilizer. Keep the soil evenly moist during bloom time. After blooming, the plant needs a rest period, so water sparingly then. 'Picotee' generally blooms again in about three months. Propagate by division.

$\mathcal{W}$AX BEGONIA
Begonia Semperflorens-Cultorum hybrid

- ✂ **Small plant**
- ✂ **Many flowers**
- ✂ **Tolerates neglect**

Today's wax begonias flower freely in white and in many shades of red and pink. (Older varieties were small and not too attractive.) The waxy leaves come in burgundy, bright green, dark green, and variegated with white. For quick color the wax begonia is tough to beat, and some varieties are almost everblooming indoors. Plants are small, so you should grow several in a decorative pot for greater impact.

Grow wax begonias in a bright location in rich soil kept evenly moist all year. Feed monthly with 10-10-10 fertilizer. Trim back the foliage occasionally, and keep plants out of drafts. Propagate by division.

$\mathcal{M}$APLE-LEAF BEGONIA
Begonia superba 'Rana'

- ✂ **Large plant**
- ✂ **Handsome foliage**
- ✂ **Easy to grow**

The unusual reddish brown foliage of the 'Rana' maple-leaf begonia makes it one of the handsomest in this huge family. A tall, upright plant, it has a decorative appearance for interiors. The pink flowers borne in winter are another asset.

Plant 'Rana' in evenly moist all-purpose soil, and place it in an airy location with some sun. Feed quarterly with 10-10-10 fertilizer, and prune away lower leaves as the plant matures. Produce new plants by division.

Bromeliads (BROMELIACEAE)

 ## Urn Plant
Aechmea fasciata

- Medium size
- Long-lasting floral bracts
- Good room decoration

With stiff, arching leaves that have undersides frosted with silvery scales, urn plant is the most popular bromeliad. Like its cousin, silver urn plant (shown below), urn plant has a crown of pink bracts that lasts for months surrounding tiny blue flowers. Most kinds of urn plant have frosted mottled green foliage.

Grow urn plant in a bright location, and pot it in fine-grade fir bark. Keep the plant's "urn" filled with water, and change it weekly. Keep the fir bark slightly moist. Maintain moderate temperatures, and do not fertilize. Two misconceptions about this and other bromeliads are that putting an apple inside the urn will make them bloom and that insects will gather in the urn when grown indoors. Neither is true. Propagate from offsets.

 ## Silver Urn Plant
Aechmea chantinii hybrid

- Large plant
- Long-lasting floral bracts
- Easy to grow

Urn plants originated in South America and are named for their "urn" of leaves that catches water. Their genus name, *Aechmea*, is derived from the Greek, meaning "spear point." Indeed, the plants have stiff, pointed leaves and tiny blue flowers surrounded by pointed, stiff pink bracts.

Grow urn plants in a bright location but out of direct sun. The plant does best in a mix of equal parts potting soil and fine-grade fir bark kept evenly moist. Always keep the "urn" of the plant filled with water, and change it weekly. Do not fertilize. Maintain moderate temperatures that never drop below 55°F at night. Keep the plant in its pot until the flowers fade, and then let it die naturally. Start new plants from offsets. See also urn plant, above.

VARIEGATED PINEAPPLE PLANT

Ananas cosmosus 'Variegatus'

- Dwarf to large varieties
- Novelty plant
- Not easy to grow

Spanish conquistadores discovered pineapple plant in South America in the early 1700s, and European royalty enjoyed eating the sweet, exotic fruit. Pineapple plants are slow growing and fussy about conditions. Variegated pineapple plant, shown here, has leaves colored in a blend of green, cream, and sometimes red. It bears blue flowers and nonedible bitter red fruit. The species' standard size is large and spiny when mature, so also look for the dwarf species, *Ananas nanus*, which grows to about 15 inches tall.

Grow pineapple plants in fine-grade fir bark, and keep the center of the plant filled with water. As with other bromeliads, change the water in the urn every week. This plant is fussy about cultivation but is an attractive novelty. Start new plants from offsets.

FANTASIA BROMELIAD

Billbergia 'Fantasia'

- Medium size
- Long-lasting flower crown
- Easy to grow

This bromeliad hybrid appears frequently in collections because it is free flowering and easy to grow. It has a purple-and-red inflorescence, or flower cluster, and leaves mottled with cream. This tube-shaped, vertical plant grows to 30 inches tall. Although not as spectacular as some bromeliads, it is dependable.

Grow 'Fantasia' bromeliad in fine-grade fir bark, and keep the medium evenly moist but never soggy. Do not fertilize. Provide a bright location out of direct sun, and keep temperatures above 50°F at night. Propagate from offsets.

Bromeliads cont'd

EARTH STAR
Cryptanthus species and hybrids

* Small plant
* Colorful foliage
* Easy to grow

The plants in the genus *Cryptanthus* are small (to 14 inches in diameter). New cultivars constantly appear, one more colorful than the other. Grow these plants for their crinkly leaves. 'Tricolor' has the star-shaped rosette form and slender leaves that are strikingly tri-colored: green, white, and pink.

Earth stars respond to basic care. Give them bright light without direct sun to fully develop the foliage color. Pot earth stars in equal parts potting soil and fine-grade fir bark, and grow them in small pots because the plants like to be potbound. Keep the soil evenly moist, and fertilize quarterly with 20-10-10 fertilizer. Start new plants from offsets.

ORANGE STAR BROMELIAD
Guzmania lingulata 'Orange Star'

* Medium size
* Long lasting floral bracts
* Easy to grow

From South America, the genus Guzmania comprises some 70 species, many of which are stellar houseplants. 'Orange Star' grows in a rosette, almost fan-shaped, form to about 24 inches across. Orange bracts that stay colorful for five months encircle the small, white, true flowers in the plant's center.

Guzmanias like a bright location out of direct sun. They thrive in a mix of equal parts fine-grade fir bark and potting soil. Keep the medium evenly moist, and change the water in the urn weekly. Do not fertilize. Plants bloom once and then die but produce many small offsets, which you can propagate.

$\mathcal{R}$ANA BROMELIAD

Guzmania lingulata 'Rana'

- ❦ **Medium size**
- ❦ **Elegant appearance**
- ❦ **Colorful at bloom time**

This new Guzmania hybrid has somewhat larger flower heads than the species, and its fine green foliage grows in an attractive rosette. The plant grows to 30 inches tall. It thrives under the average temperature and humidity conditions of most homes and rarely needs attention. Wipe the leaves with a damp cloth to keep plant healthy.

Give 'Rana' a bright location out of direct sun. Plant this bromeliad in fine-grade fir bark, and keep it evenly moist. Keep water in the plant's center, and remember to change the water weekly. Propagate from offsets. See Chapter 6, "Propagating Houseplants," page 85, for detailed instruction on dividing offsets from bromeliads.

$\mathcal{P}$OKER PLANT

Guzmania zahnii

- ❦ **Medium size**
- ❦ **Compact fountainlike growth**
- ❦ **Easy to grow**

The tall flower spike of this handsome small plant from Brazil rises from the plant's center covered with tiny yellow flowers. The plant stays in bloom for many weeks and makes a good table accent. It grows to 24 inches across.

Grow in a bright location out of direct sun. Plant in fir bark, and keep the medium evenly moist all year. Keep plant's center filled with water, and change the water weekly. Do not fertilize. Propagate from offsets.

Bromeliads cont'd

S TRIPED NEOREGELIA
Neoregelia carolinae forma *tricolor*

- **Medium size**
- **Stunning color**
- **Easy to grow**

This South American bromeliad appeared in cultivation about 1940 and created a sensation with its handsome multicolored leaves and bright red flower bracts. The leaves—striped with green, creamy white, and pink—grow in a compact rosette to 28 inches. At bloom time, the leaves near the plant's center turn bright red. Best of all, this plant is easy to grow. Display it on a low table, so its striking colors can be seen easily.

Provide a bright sunny location. Grow the plant in a mix of equal parts fine-grade fir bark and potting soil, and keep the mix moderately moist all year. Feed twice a year with 20-10-10 fertilizer. Propagate from offsets, which form at the base.

R OYAL BURGUNDY BROMELIAD
Neoregelia 'Royal Burgundy'

- **Medium size**
- **Extraordinary leaf color**
- **Easy to grow**

Unlike many other bromeliads, neoregelias are grown primarily for their handsome leaves. This decorative hybrid has burgundy-colored foliage and grows to about 36 inches tall. Because it needs little attention, this is a good bromeliad for beginners.

Give 'Royal Burgundy' a bright location with some sun to produce good foliage color, and plant it in fine-grade fir bark. Water sparingly so that the planting medium is barely moist all year. Keep the center of the plant filled with water, and change the water monthly. Start new plants from offsets.

ℬLUSHING BROMELIAD
Neoregelia hybrid

❧ **Medium size**
❧ **Handsome foliage**
❧ **Fine interior decorative plant**

This neoregelia from Brazil has stunning leaves blotched green and red. Growing in a rosette form, the plant has the tubular central urn typical of bromeliads and grows to 30 inches tall.

Give this bromeliad a place in bright light but without direct sun. Use a potting medium of fine-grade fir bark. The root system is small, so water sparingly, keeping the bark barely moist all year. Keep the plant's urn filled with water, and change the water weekly. Do not fertilize. Start new plants from offsets.

ℱINGERNAIL PLANT
Neoregelia spectabilis

❧ **Medium size**
❧ **Leaves bright red at center**
❧ **Easy to grow**

The center and tips of this Brazilian native's leaves turn scarlet at bloom time, the tips inspiring the painted fingernail image in the common name. Small violet flowers are hidden deep in the center.

Grow in bright conditions, found near east- and south-facing windows. Pot in fine-grade fir bark, and keep the bark evenly moist. Do not fertilize. The plant does best in normal household temperatures that never drop below 60°F. Propagate from offsets.

ℙLUME BROMELIAD
Tillandsia cyanea

❧ **Small to medium size**
❧ **Handsome pink bracts**
❧ **Easy to grow**

With a low rosette of narrow green leaves and a pink plumelike flower stalk that bears large, short-lived violet-purple flowers, plume bromeliad commands attention. This Ecuadorian plant was once available only in a large size, to about 40 inches. Now there are dwarf cultivars to 10 inches.

Grow this plant in a bright location out of direct sun. Plant in small pots in fine-grade fir bark. Keep the bark medium moist but never soggy. Maintain normal household temperatures. Feed twice a year with 20-20-10 fertilizer. Propagate from offsets.

Bromeliads cont'd

TUFTED BROMELIAD
Tillandsia ionantha

- Small epiphytic plant
- Colorful foliage
- Easy to grow—even foolproof

Forming a tiny fountain of grayish green leaves, the center of which turns blood red at bloom time in summer, this little bromeliad is not to be missed. It's an epiphyte, meaning that its roots take moisture and nutrients from the air rather than from soil. Like other epiphytes, this one grows best wired to a piece of wood. It grows to only about 4 inches in diameter and is a fascinating conversation piece.

Tufted bromeliad needs a sunny place and does best when misted with water almost daily. It does not grow well in a pot. Instead, choose a piece of branch or wood of some type to support it. Wire the plant in place; eventually it will take hold. Do not fertilize. Start new plants from offsets.

YELLOW POKER PLANT
Vriesea hybrid

- Grows easily to 30 inches
- Beautiful yellow plume-like flower heads
- Dramatic color

This vriesea hybrid bears an exotic tri-colored yellow flower head on which the inflorescence, or flower cluster, stays fresh for many weeks.

Grow yellow poker plant in a bright, somewhat sunny location. Pot it in fine-grade fir bark. Keep the center of the plant filled with water, and be sure to change the water weekly. Do not fertilize the yellow poker plant. Propagate new plants from offsets.

Note: Flower heads remain in color for many weeks and in time dry naturally on the plant. The flower heads can then be cut and used in long-lasting dried flower arrangements.

138
PLANT PROFILES

$\mathcal{P}$OELMANII FLAMING SWORD
Vriesea × poelmanii

- ❧ **Small to medium-size plant**
- ❧ **Fiery red flower bracts**
- ❧ **Colorful for months**

A large, fiery red, narrow plumelike flower head makes this bromeliad from South America a popular choice. The plant grows to about 24 inches.

Grow flaming sword in a sunny location, and pot it in fine-grade fir bark. The plant will also grow on a chunk of tree branch or a slab of bark. Water frequently in warm weather, and keep the central urn of the plant filled with water, but change it weekly. Feeding is not really necessary, but the plant likes good ventilation. Start new plants from offsets that form at the base of the plant.

$\mathcal{F}$LAMING SWORD
Vriesea splendens

- ❧ **Medium size**
- ❧ **Long lasting flower head**
- ❧ **Easy to grow**

Flaming sword bears a distinctive reddish orange sword-shaped flower cluster on an erect stem. This plant has been popular since the late nineteenth century, and today there are countless hybrids.

Flaming sword can tolerate low light, but does best in bright light. Pot it in fine-grade fir bark, and keep the bark evenly moist all year. Like other vrieseas, flaming sword prefers warm conditions in which the temperature never drops below 60°F at night. Keep the center of the plant filled with water, and change the water weekly. Propagate from offsets.

Other good species: *V. × mariae, V. schwackeana*

Cacti and Succulents (Various Families)

Desert Rose
Adenium obesum

- **Medium size**
- **Pretty pink flowers**
- **Easy to grow**

The unusual treelike shape and clusters of handsome pink flowers in summer make this succulent particularly desirable. Desert rose has an attractive branching growth habit and grows to 30 inches. It deserves to be more widely used in homes.

Grow desert rose in bright light in a mix of equal parts potting soil and sharp sand. Keep the medium barely moist all year—this plant does not tolerate overwatering. Feed quarterly with 10-10-10 fertilizer. Don't attempt to propagate new plants at home; instead, purchase them from suppliers.

Peanut Cactus
Chamaecereus sylvestrii (aka *Echinopsis chamaecereus*)

- **Small plant**
- **Fine red flowers**
- **Easy to grow**

Originally from Argentina, peanut cactus is fast-growing and blooms easily indoors. It forms a clump of branching, columnar stems that grow to 20 inches and are covered with soft spines. On a young plant, the stems look like peanuts. Orange-red flowers appear in summer.

Place peanut cactus in a warm, sunny location. Grow in a mix of equal parts sharp sand and potting soil kept evenly moist. Use small pots for best growth. Feed twice a year with 20-10-10 fertilizer. Repot the plant only occasionally, because it takes time to recover after being disturbed. Propagate from offsets.

Jade Tree
Crassula ovata (aka *Crassula argentea*)

- **Medium size**
- **Leaves resemble small pieces of jade**
- **Easy to grow**

This wonderful bushlike plant grows to 30 inches or more over time. If given enough light, jade plant bears small whitish flowers in summer. Large plants in decorative containers are quite attractive.

Grow in a bright location, and pot in standard houseplant soil. Keep the soil somewhat dry all year. Feed quarterly with 20-10-10 fertilizer. Occasionally clean the leaves using a damp cloth. Propagate from leaf cuttings.

FALSE ROSE
Echeveria hybrid

- ❧ Small plant
- ❧ Handsome roselike growth
- ❧ Easy to grow

Many echeverias have flowers resembling small open-faced roses in shades of pink or yellow. This unnamed hybrid has bronze gold leaves in a small rosette to 12 inches across. It's perfect as a table decoration and doesn't need much attention.

Grow in a mix of equal parts sharp sand and potting

soil kept barely moist all year. Keep in bright light but out of direct sun. Feed quarterly with 20-20-10 fertilizer. Propagate from offsets.

CROWN-OF-THORNS
Euphorbia milii

- ❧ Thorny medium-size plant
- ❧ Small red flowers
- ❧ Blooms in winter

This unusual-looking poinsettia relative from Africa commands attention, especially in winter, when it blooms abundantly. Dense and shrubby, the plant has thorny stems but offers fine green color and red, pink, or yellow flowers.

Grow near a bright window. Plant in a 6- or 8-inch pot, and use equal parts sharp sand and potting soil. Keep the mix evenly moist all year, especially during the fall. Keep water away from the leaves. Feed quarterly with 20-20-10 fertilizer, and never allow the temperature to drop below 60°F at night. Propagate from stem cuttings.

WAX PLANT, PORCELAIN FLOWER
Hoya carnosa

- ❧ Very large
- ❧ Available in many improved cultivars
- ❧ Easy to grow, thrives on neglect

The wax plant is really a vine with deep green succulent leaves and clusters of waxy, honey-scented white to pale pink flowers with red crowns, which may drip nectar. The plant needs time to adjust when you bring it home, but don't give up on it, for it may not bloom lavishly until two or three years old.

Wax plant needs full sun to bloom and blooms best when potbound. Don't remove the stem, or spur, on which the flowers have been produced because it's the source of next season's bloom. Grow in standard all-purpose houseplant soil. Water plentifully in spring and summer but not as much in winter, when the soil can be allowed to become quite dry. Propagate from stem, leaf, or tip cuttings taken in spring.

Cacti and Succulents cont'd

 ## Felt Bush, Velvet Leaf
Kalanchoe beharensis

- Medium size to large
- Interesting leaves
- Tolerates neglect

Mostly native to Madagascar and Africa, this kalanchoe is dubbed teddy bear plant because its thick leaves are softly fuzzy. Decorative year-round, it can grow to 40 inches.

Plant in a bright location. This plant needs a somewhat sandy soil, so add some sharp sand to standard houseplant soil. Water evenly all year, but keep the soil dryish, never allowing it to become very wet. Keep water away from leaves, or they will rot. Feed every third month with 10-10-10 fertilizer. Propagate from leaf cuttings.

 ## Starfire Kalanchoe
Kalanchoe blossfeldiana

- Small plant
- Available in several colors
- Can bloom twice a year

With succulent green leaves and pretty bunches of red, orange, yellow, or beige flowers that bloom twice yearly, starfire kalanchoe is a winning houseplant.

Provide bright light. Grow in a 6- or 8-inch pot of standard all-purpose houseplant soil. Keep the soil evenly moist except after bloom. Then, in order to force another flush of flowers, decrease watering and do not fertilize for at least six to eight weeks. This kalanchoe likes average household temperatures. Start new plants from stem cuttings.

 ## Dinner-plate Kalanchoe
Kalanchoe thyrsiflora

- Medium size
- Exquisitely colored leaves
- Highly recommended

The succulent greenish gray, red-tinged leaves of this unusual-looking plant from South Africa are as large as dinner plates. This plant grows to 24 inches tall and offers a lot of color.

Dinner-plate kalanchoe thrives in bright light. Plant it in a potting mix of equal parts houseplant soil and sharp sand. Keep the medium evenly moist, but do not overwater. Feed quarterly with 20-10-10 fertilizer. The plant tolerates temperatures down to 55°F at night. Since propagation is difficult at home, purchase new plants from suppliers instead.

Globe Cactus

Mammillaria celsiana (aka Mammillaria muehlenpfordtii)

✤ **Small plant**
✤ **Globe-shaped**
✤ **Easy to grow**

Sculptural and globe-shaped, this durable Mexican native is covered with short yellow spines. In summer, purplish red flowers appear. Globe cactus grows to only 4 inches tall and about 5 inches in diameter.

Grow globe cactus in a bright window. If the plant receives sun, it may reward you with rosy blooms. Plant in a mix of equal parts potting soil and sharp sand; keep the medium just moist, never really wet or dry. Feed every three months with 20-10-10 fertilizer. Propagate from offsets.

Pachyphytum Plant
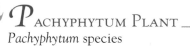

Pachyphytum species

✤ **Medium size**
✤ **Bright green succulent leaves**
✤ **Easy to grow**

This handsome, slow-growing succulent has pale green, almond-shaped, thick leaves. A compact plant, it grows to 30 inches tall and looks good in a hanging basket. If you don't find this plant when shopping, inquire about ordering it. It's a reliable performer that survives neglect.

Pachyphytums need dappled sunlight. Plant in standard all-purpose potting soil that drains well. Allow the soil to dry out between waterings. Feed only twice a year, in spring and summer, with 20-10-10 fertilizer. Propogate new plants from stem cuttings.

Cacti and Succulents cont'd

Ball Cactus

Parodia penicillata

- Small plant
- Orange-red flowers
- Easy to grow

From Argentina and Bolivia, this globular plant with light-colored spines sports handsome orange-red flowers in summer that emerge from the top of the "ball" but last only a few days. This 6-inch cactus makes a good table or desk accent.

Grow in a sunny location in equal parts potting soil and sharp sand that drains well. Keep the medium somewhat moist but never soggy. Feed twice a year with 20-10-10 fertilizer. Propagate from offsets.

Easter Cactus

Rhipsalidopsis rosea (aka *Hatiora rosea*)

- Medium size
- Spring blooming
- Abundant flowers

Nineteenth-century plant collectors discovered this plant in the rain forests of South America. It does its ancestors proud. Easter cactus is a stellar performer that produces dozens of small cerise flowers in spring. Growing to 24 inches high, these plants have gracefully arching stems composed of flat oblong segments. This is a jungle cactus, not a desert type, so it needs different growing conditions than those required by cacti from arid environments.

Grow Easter cactus in bright light but out of direct sun. Pot in organically rich soil that contains some humus. Water the soil evenly all year, but decrease watering for a few weeks after blooming to let the plant rest. Keep humidity high by misting with water daily. Routine care will bring another bloom of flowers in a year's time. Feed monthly with 10-20-10 fertilizer. Propagate from cuttings.

Pencil Cactus

Rhipsalis species

- Medium size
- Succulent, pencil-thin leaves
- Easy to grow

These exotic-looking jungle cacti have slender upright or trailing stems, that look best in hanging baskets. In their native habitat, these epiphytic plants grow directly on tree bark.

Provide pencil cactus a location with dappled sunlight, similar to the light filtering through overhead trees in a jungle. Plant in equal parts potting soil and fine-grade fir bark kept just barely moist all year. Do not overwater. Feed quarterly with 20-10-10 fertilizer. Propagate by division.

CHRISTMAS CACTUS
Schlumbergera × buckleyi (aka *Zygocactus*)

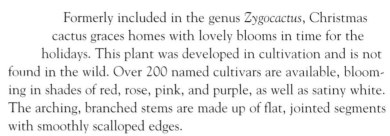

❧ **Small to medium-size plant**
❧ **Seasonal blooms**
❧ **Easy to grow**

Formerly included in the genus *Zygocactus*, Christmas cactus graces homes with lovely blooms in time for the holidays. This plant was developed in cultivation and is not found in the wild. Over 200 named cultivars are available, blooming in shades of red, rose, pink, and purple, as well as satiny white. The arching, branched stems are made up of flat, jointed segments with smoothly scalloped edges.

Christmas cactus prefers reasonably bright light from an eastern exposure, with a bit of direct sun in winter. Plant in a mix of equal parts potting soil and fine-grade fir bark, and keep the medium evenly moist all year. The plant does best in normal household temperatures and needs cool nights (to 55°F) for buds to develop. Feed monthly with 20-10-10 fertilizer. You don't need to keep the plant in the dark to encourage blooming. Keeping it away from artificial light at night for a few months prior to the holiday should be sufficient to promote flowering. Propagate from cuttings.

THANKSGIVING CACTUS
Schlumbergera truncata

❧ **Small to medium-size plant**
❧ **Seasonal blooms**
❧ **Easy to grow**

Thanksgiving cactus is epiphytic, growing on trees in the jungles of Brazil. In fall, multitudes of brightly colored red, rose, or pink flowers bloom at the tips of the stems.

Thanksgiving cactus needs bright light from an eastern exposure, with some direct sun in winter. Plant in a mix of equal parts potting soil and fine-grade fir bark, and keep the medium evenly moist all year. Provide normal household temperatures. Feed monthly with 20-10-10 fertilizer. To promote Thanksgiving flowering, keep away from artificial light at night a few months prior to the holiday. Propagate from cuttings.

Cacti and Succulents cont'd

Donkey's Tail
Sedum morganianum

* Medium-size to large plant
* Cascading leaves
* Easy to grow

The weight of this plant's succulent leaves causes mature branches to cascade like a donkey's tail. The stems of young plants are upright. If conditions are right, the plant bears small pink flowers.

Grow donkey's tail in a mix of equal parts sharp sand and potting soil, and keep the mix just barely moist. Provide full sun from a south window. Avoid placing the plant in drafts. Use a hanging container so that the stems can trail over the sides. Feed every two months with 20-20-10 fertilizer. Donkey's tail is difficult to propagate under home conditions. Buy new plants from suppliers.

Starfish Flower
Stapelia gigantea

* Medium size
* Bizarre malodorous flowers
* Handsome sculptural form

Like many succulent houseplants, starfish flower is native to South Africa. It caused a sensation when first presented for sale in the mid-nineteenth century. The star-shaped flowers are large—to 7 inches across—luridly colored and generally malodorous. Compact, the plant rarely grows more than 24 inches tall. With its handsome, dark green, grooved high columns, it's a fine plant for a windowsill. The flowers droop and usually appear in summer.

Grow starfish flower in a sunny spot. Grow in equal parts fine-grade fir bark and potting soil. Keep the medium barely moist all year; do not overwater. Feed quarterly with 10-10-10 fertilizer. Propagate by division.

Torch Cactus
Trichocereus candicans (aka *Echinocereus candicans*)

* Large plant
* Columnar
* Slow grower

From Argentina, this columnar cactus with yellow spines grows to 40 inches. It rarely flowers indoors and is used like sculpture. Many varieties are available, all similar in appearance.

Grow in a bright location, in all-purpose houseplant soil. You can add sand, but do not grow the plant only in sand. Keep the soil barely moist. Feed monthly with 10-10-10 fertilizer. Purchase new plants from suppliers.

$\mathcal{E}$uphorbia Family (EUPHORBIACEAE)

 ## $\mathcal{C}$HENILLE PLANT
Acalypha hispida

- **Excellent medium-size plant**
- **Distinctive**
- **Needs regular care**

Chenille plant thrives in a large container, producing unusual strings of tiny pinkish red flowers on and off throughout the year.

Provide a brightly lit location, with sun in winter. Grow in standard all-purpose houseplant soil, and feed monthly with 10-10-10 fertilizer. Provide high humidity and moderate temperatures. Propagate from cuttings.

$\mathcal{C}$ROTON
Codiaeum variegatum var. *pictum*

- **Medium-size to large plant**
- **Colorful foliage**
- **Needs some attention**

This sun-lover from Malaysia and southern India is known for its brightly colored foliage in various shades and combinations of green, red, orange, yellow, pink, and white.

Plant crotons in a large pot of standard all-purpose houseplant soil. Keep the soil evenly moist all year, and feed every other week with 20-10-10 fertilizer. Propagate from cuttings.

$\mathcal{P}$OINSETTIA
Euphorbia pulcherrima

- **Great medium-size to large seasonal plant**
- **Glowing red bracts**
- **Needs a dark period for 10 weeks to rebloom**

A Mexican native, the poinsettia is the traditional Christmas gift plant. Its "flowers" are really leaflike bracts that surround tiny yellow and green true flowers. Traditionally red, cultivars now come in white, pink, or streaked red and white. The plant lasts several weeks indoors and may grow to 48 inches. Most are discarded when the color fades, but rebloom is possible. Here's how:

Grow in a bright but cool location, with daytime temperatures of 65° to 70°F, dropping no lower than 50°F at night. Use standard all-purpose houseplant soil that drains readily. Keep soil evenly moist until leaves start to fall, and then water sparingly. Do not fertilize. In late March or early April, cut back severely to 6 inches, and repot in fresh soil. In summer place the plant outdoors in a shady location. After Labor Day, bring the plant inside. To initiate new buds, provide 12 hours of darkness every day for about 10 weeks prior to the holiday. Propagate from cuttings. *Caution:* The plant is poisonous, so keep it away from pets and children. Also the sap of euphorbias can cause a rash.

Ferns (Various Families)

Lacy Maidenhair Fern
Adiantum tenerum

- Small plant
- Graceful
- Somewhat difficult to grow

With delicate, lacy, light green fronds on wiry arching stems, lacy maidenhair fern is a handsome, decorative plant from Mexico and Venezuela. It has been grown indoors since the mid-nineteenth century.

Provide a bright but not sunny location. Pot it in humusy soil, and keep the soil evenly moist, never too dry or too wet. Fertilize three times a year with 20-20-10 plant food. Propagate by division.

Good cultivars: 'Wrightii', 'Pacific Maid'

Bird's Nest Fern
Asplenium nidus

- Medium-size to large plant
- Impressive when mature
- Easy to grow

Bird's nest fern produces a crown of smooth, shiny fronds with a hollow and funnel-shaped center, somewhat like a bird's nest. This native of New Zealand, tropical Asia, and Polynesia can grow large—to 4 feet in diameter—but generally stays closer to 2 feet indoors.

Grow bird's nest fern in moderate light. Use a rich potting mix of equal parts soil and humus in a large container. Keep the soil evenly moist all year. If you summer the plant outdoors, protect it from slugs and snails. (Use a snail bait without metaldehyde.) Feed every month with 10-10-5 fertilizer. Repot every third year. Propagate by seed (spores) or buy new plants.

Good cultivar: 'Elegance'

TREE FERN
Blechnum gibbum

- **Medium size**
- **Stiff green fronds**
- **Durable fern**

Also known by the botanic name *Blechnum occidentalis*, this fern from New Caledonia flourishes in the home with little care. A favorite from Victorian times, it grows slowly to 30 inches.

Plant in equal parts soil and fine-grade fir bark kept evenly moist. Place in a bright location, and feed semiannually with 20-20-10 plant food. Propagate by division.

HOLLY FERN
Cyrtomium falcatum

- **Medium size**
- **Graceful**
- **Can take neglect**

This Asian native has attractive deep green fronds with leaflets shaped somewhat like holly leaves. Unlike some ferns, it does not shed. At 30 inches, holly fern's compact size makes it ideal for many rooms.

Grow in bright light. (It will grow in dimmer conditions but won't do as well.) Plant in standard all-purpose houseplant soil, and allow the soil to dry out between waterings. Feed semiannually with 20-20-20 fertilizer. Keep holly fern out of drafts. Propagate by division.

Good cultivar: 'Rochfordianum'

JAPANESE SHIELD FERN
Dryopteris erythrosora

- **Medium-size, compact plant**
- **Bright green color**
- **Elegant appearance**

Seldom seen indoors, though it makes a fine houseplant, this slow grower has a neat branching habit and graceful appearance. It is native to China and Japan.

Grow in moderately bright light without direct sun. Pot in humusy soil that drains well, and keep the soil evenly moist. Feed quarterly with 10-20-10 fertilizer. Propagate by division.

Ferns cont'd

Fluffy Ruffles Boston Fern
Nephrolepis exaltata 'Fluffy Ruffles'

- Medium-size to large plant
- Lovely in a hanging basket
- Grows in bright light or shade

The classic Boston fern species, which originated in Africa, remains a favorite. Today there are innumerable cultivars, including 'Fluffy Ruffles' (shown). These cultivars are sturdier than the species. Some can grow to 60 inches in diameter with arching fronds. The one drawback is their tendency to drop leaflets, which can look untidy.

Grow in a bright location without direct sun, and use humusy soil—add extra humus to standard all-purpose houseplant soil. Feed twice a year with 20-20-20 fertilizer. For best results, repot annually in fresh soil. Propagate by division.

Another good cultivar: 'Dallasii'

Timii Nephrolepis
Nephrolepis exaltata 'Timii'

- Small to medium-size fern
- Fine table accent
- Easy to grow

This Boston fern cultivar is small—rarely growing over 30 inches—and its fronds are similar to those of the Boston fern but somewhat bushier. This graceful plant makes a lovely accent on a table or desk.

'Timii' likes a bright but not sunny place. Plant this fern in a well-draining soil rich with organic matter. Feed a few times a year with 10-20-10 fertilizer. Start new plants by division.

Button Fern
Pellaea rotundifolia

- Small plant
- Low growing, trailing
- Easy to grow

With arching, trailing fronds composed of small, round, green leaflets, this New Zealand native has a tropical look.

Grow in bright light without direct sun. Button fern needs good drainage, so add some perlite or sand to the soil mix. Keep the soil moist, but avoid overwatering. Feed monthly with 20-20-10 fertilizer. Repot every second year in fresh soil. Propagation from spores is difficult. Instead, purchase new plants.

CABBAGE HEAD FERN
Polypodium vulgare (aka *Polypody*)

- ☘ **Medium size to large**
- ☘ **Compact growth**
- ☘ **Lush green fronds**

A fast-growing plant with large scalloped leaves and, when mature, fuzzy brown rhizomes, this fern is native to Europe, eastern Asia, and North America. It can grow to 48 inches. If you have the space, cabbage head fern

makes a striking room accent in a large decorative container.

Grow this fern in moderate light, and pot it in a mix of equal parts fine-grade fir bark and potting soil. Keep the soil evenly moist all year. Feed monthly with 20-10-10 fertilizer. A difficult fern, this one dislikes drafts and overwatering. Propagate by division.

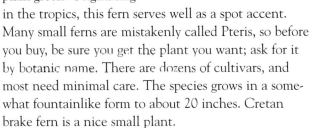

CRETAN BRAKE FERN
Pteris cretica

- ☘ **Small fern**
- ☘ **Decorative accent**
- ☘ **Easy to grow**

Cretan brake fern fronds are small and may be multicolored or striped with silver, as well as plain green. Originating in the tropics, this fern serves well as a spot accent. Many small ferns are mistakenly called Pteris, so before you buy, be sure you get the plant you want; ask for it by botanic name. There are dozens of cultivars, and most need minimal care. The species grows in a somewhat fountainlike form to about 20 inches. Cretan brake fern is a nice small plant.

Grow Cretan brake fern in bright to moderate light without direct sun, in a rich, humusy soil. Keep the soil evenly moist all year, and feed every other month with 10-10-10 fertilizer. Start new plants by division.

 LEATHER FERN
Rumohra adiantiformis

- ☘ **Medium size**
- ☘ **Attractive leathery green fronds**
- ☘ **Good hanging plant**

Leather fern is a tough, robust plant. The fronds can grow to 36 inches, and the plant has an airy appearance. It provides a refreshing change from the common Boston fern. As it matures, it looks better in hanging baskets.

Grow in a bright window. Use a mix of equal parts potting soil and humus, and keep it moist all year. Feed monthly with 20-20-10 fertilizer. Propagate by division.

Gesneriads (GESNERIACEAE)

Lipstick Plant
Aeschynanthus species

- 𝒴 **Large trailing plant**
- 𝒴 **Lovely flowers**
- 𝒴 **Tolerates neglect**

There are many species and cultivars of aeschynanthus, some with blackish green leaves, others with bright green leaves; some have red flowers, and others have brownish red or orange flowers. The tubular blossoms, resembling lipstick in a tube, inspired the common name for this plant. The trailing stems grow to 48 inches.

Grow this plant in a bright location with some direct sun, especially in winter. Plant in all-purpose potting soil, and keep it evenly moist all year. Provide good air circulation. Feed about once a month with 20-10-10 fertilizer. Propagate from cuttings.

Button Columnea
Columnea arguta

- 𝒴 **Large, excellent trailer**
- 𝒴 **Abundant flowers**
- 𝒴 **Dense foliage**

If you come across this spectacular performer from Central America, buy it. With small button-shaped leaves and orange flowers that appear for six months on stems growing to 48 inches long, this exotic, elegant trailer should be displayed in a hanging basket.

Grow button columnea in a bright, airy location. Water about three times a week and feed monthly with 10-30-10 fertilizer. To encourage blooming, provide a three-week winter rest by reducing watering and not fertilizing. The plant does well in average house temperatures that never drop below 50°F. Propagate from cuttings.

Flame Violet
Episcia cupreata

- 𝒴 **Small trailer**
- 𝒴 **Blooms in spring**
- 𝒴 **Likes warmth**

This South American native has leaves that combine shades of deep green, mahogany, brown, and copper, with contrasting veins of silver or light green. Tubular flowers in red, yellow, orange, and pink bloom in spring.

Place flame violet out of drafts, near a bright window. Use standard all-purpose soil that drains readily. Keep the soil evenly moist, but avoid wetting the leaves. Feed monthly with 10-30-10 fertilizer. Grow in a small pot. Repot every second year in fresh soil. Propagate from cuttings or offsets.

Good cultivars: 'Acajou', 'Cygnet', 'Emerald Queen'

Goldfish Plant

Nematanthus gregarius (aka *Hypocyrta nummularia*)

- ❧ **Medium size**
- ❧ **Bright shiny foliage**
- ❧ **Easy to grow**

This Central American plant has trailing stems to 30 inches long, lined with glossy deep green oval leaves. The pouchlike orange flowers resemble goldfish and generally bloom during warm months.

Grow goldfish plant in a bright location, ideally an east window. Pot in standard all-purpose potting soil. Water freely all year except in winter. Feed monthly with 20-20-10 plant food, except when the plant is resting. Generally, it goes dormant in winter and after flowering but eventually starts growing again. When the plant rests, withhold fertilizer, and cut back on watering until new growth begins. Grow in a hanging basket. Repot every second year. Start new plants from stem or tip cuttings.

Good cultivars: 'Tropicana', 'Black Gold'

African Violet

Saintpaulia cultivars

- ❧ **Small plant**
- ❧ **Longtime favorite**
- ❧ **Flowers in many colors**

Miniature, dwarf, and standard-size African violets come in many flower types and colors and may grow in a neat rosette or have trailing stems. Flowers may be single, double, edged with white (picotee), fringed, or star-shaped. Flower colors may be blue-violet, purple, pink, dark red, and white, as well as bicolored. Grown from nine species found throughout Africa, today's hybrids all have the typical cup-shaped, somewhat hairy leaves and clusters of small, pretty flowers. Given enough light, they bloom practically year-round.

Provide African violets good winter sunlight (and bright light in summer) and night temperatures above 55°F. Pot in standard all-purpose potting soil that drains well, and feed monthly with 10-10-10 fertilizer. Let the soil surface dry a bit between waterings. Avoid spilling water on leaves, or they'll spot. Propagate from leaf cuttings.

Gesneriads cont'd

Gloxinia

Sinningia hybrid

- Medium size
- Stunning large flowers
- Excellent gift plant

The large, ruffled, trumpet-shaped flowers of gloxinia come in a stunning range of colors—violet, cardinal red, purple, pink, and white, some edged, blotched, or streaked with a contrasting color. The blooms are carried on slender stems above a rosette of large, broadly oval deep green leaves. Gloxinia hybrids are descended from a plant native to South America. Their dramatic flowers open in spring, but good care can keep them blooming indoors for several months. Given a cool, dark, dormant period, the tubers may rebloom, but most people use gloxinia as a seasonal plant and then discard it.

Grow Gloxinia in bright but filtered light in a location near a south or east window covered by a sheer curtain. Pot in all-purpose potting soil, and feed weekly with 10-20-10 fertilizer. Keep the soil evenly moist while the plant is growing and blooming. *Here's how to make the plant rebloom:* When growth stops, withhold water until the foliage dies. Remove leaves, and store the tuber in a cool, dry place. Barely moisten the soil every few weeks. When you see new growth, repot the tuber in fresh soil. Leave only the sprout exposed, and place the pot in bright light. If your gloxinia originally grew from a tuber, it may not go dormant.

Temple Bells

Smithiantha speciosus

- Unusual small to medium-size plant
- Pretty orange-red flowers
- Impressive mature specimens

With small, pretty flowers that bloom off and on throughout the year, this handsome but often overlooked plant grows to about 24 inches.

For this gesneriad, a bright location is ideal. Use an all-purpose potting soil that drains readily, and keep the soil well watered. If the plant is allowed to dry out, it quickly succumbs. Feed monthly with 10-10-10 fertilizer. Propagate by division.

STREPTOCARPELLA CAPE PRIMROSE
Streptocarpus hybrid (subgenus *Streptocarpella*)

- **Medium-size hanging plant**
- **Small purple flowers**
- **Bushy growth**

Flowers in shades of violet and purple bloom off and on year-round on plants in this trailing hybrid. Mature plants grow to 30 inches in diameter.

Grow in bright light, in a hanging basket. Pot in humusy soil that drains readily. Keep the soil moist, and feed monthly with 10-10-10 fertilizer. The plant sends out errant stems, but light pruning keeps it handsome. Propagate by division.

CAPE PRIMROSE
Streptocarpus hybrid

- **Small plant**
- **Colorful flowers**
- **Likes moderate temperatures**

The trumpet-shaped flowers of Cape primrose are borne on slender stems above a cluster of fairly large fuzzy leaves. Flower colors of this native to South Africa and Madagascar now range from purple, mauve, and pink to white. Cape primroses are fine decorative plants, with one flower following another in early spring to summer. Compact hybrids rarely grow higher than 18 inches.

Grow Cape primrose in a bright location with plenty of winter sun. Pot in a well-drained all-purpose potting soil. The plant can tolerate temperatures as low as 55°F at night. Fertilize monthly with 10-20-10 fertilizer. Propagate by division or leaf cuttings.

Good cultivars: 'Bright Eyes', 'Dark Shadow', 'Fireworks', 'Midnight Flame', 'Moonlight', and 'Nightingale'

Ginger Family (ZINGIBERACEAE)

❀ ORANGE TULIP
Costus curvibracteatus

- ❀ Medium size
- ❀ Pretty little orange flowers
- ❀ Handsome bushy growth

If you want tropical beauty, buy this ginger relative. It is densely covered with handsome green leaves arranged in a spiral pattern around the stem. At the stem tips, small orange flowers bloom periodically through the warm months. A decorative plant well suited to indoor culture, orange tulip is becoming more widely available from mail-order suppliers.

Provide sunshine, water, and moderate temperatures. Use all-purpose potting soil, and feed monthly with 20-30-10 fertilizer. The plant dislikes being disturbed, so keep in the same pot for several years. Topdress annually with fresh soil. Propagate by division, or purchase new plants from mail-order suppliers.

❀ CREPE PAPER FLOWER
Costus cuspidatus (C. igneus)

- ❀ Medium size
- ❀ Brilliant flower display
- ❀ Easy to grow

This Brazilian native offers dramatic fan-shaped orange flowers, with a crepe paperlike texture, that bloom in winter, one a day. With handsome dark green foliage, the plant grows to 30 inches tall. Grow in a bright but not sunny location, and pot in standard all-purpose houseplant soil. Water evenly all year. Feed at every other watering with 10-20-10 fertilizer. Propagate by division.

❀ SIAM TULIP
Curcuma alismatifolia

- ❀ Small to medium-size plant
- ❀ Exotic flowers
- ❀ Easy to grow

Flowers of curcuma are usually pinkish violet and very pretty, set off by dark green leaves. Siam tulip makes a fine pot plant and can also be used as a cut flower. The parent species is native to Thailand.

Start rhizomes in spring for summer bloom. Plant in well-drained humusy soil, and place in bright light. Do not feed. Purchase rhizomes from suppliers to start new plants.

Java Tulip

Curcuma species

- ❧ **Small to medium-size plant**
- ❧ **Exotic flower head**
- ❧ **Tuliplike foliage**

This beautiful plant is a spectacle in bloom, with pink bracts hiding tiny yellow and violet flowers. Two of the most popular common names for this plant are Java tulip and hidden ginger.

Grow in a bright but not sunny location. Use humusy potting soil. Keep the plant well watered in the warm months. During cool months, starting around November, decrease watering to allow the leaves to die back naturally so that the plant can rest for three months. Repot the rhizomes in fresh soil each year. Purchase new rhizomes from suppliers.

 ## White Dragon Butterfly Ginger

Globba winitti 'White Dragon'

- ❧ **Colorful medium-size plant**
- ❧ **White butterfly flowers**
- ❧ **Fussy about conditions**

This pretty ginger is from Thailand. Recently available commercially, it grows to about 30 inches tall and has a sprawling habit.

Butterfly ginger is somewhat temperamental and sensitive to drafts and cold. Provide bright light in a warm and somewhat humid location. Grow in humusy soil that drains readily, and keep the soil evenly moist all year. Feed bimonthly with 20-10-10 fertilizer. Purchase new plants from suppliers.

Resurrection Lily

Kaempferia rotunda

- ❧ **Attractive medium-size plant**
- ❧ **Exotic appearance**
- ❧ **Handsome foliage**

Native to India, the resurrection lily is cultivated in Java for its edible roots, but in North America it is used as a decorative indoor plant. It has white flowers and a handsome fountainlike growth habit. Its dark green leaves are splotched with darker green. The plant grows to about 36 inches tall.

Grow resurrection lily in a sunny location, in humusy, well-drained soil. Keep the soil evenly moist, and feed quarterly with 10-20-10 fertilizer. Purchase new plants from suppliers.

Lily Family and Relatives (LILIACEAE)

ALOE
Aloe bellatula

- **Medium-size to large plant**
- **Orange flowers**
- **Easy to grow**

This fine aloe from South Africa has narrow, spiky, succulent leaves with toothed edges. In the warm months the plant bears long stems topped with small orange flowers.

Grow aloe in bright light. Use all-purpose potting soil that drains readily. Keep the soil evenly moist all year. Feed quarterly with 10-10-10 fertilizer. Because this aloe prefers not to be disturbed, repot only when the plant outgrows its pot. Propagate from offsets.

HEALING ALOE, MEDICINE PLANT
Aloe vera (aka *A. barbadensis*)

- **Small to medium-size plant**
- **Popular healing plant**
- **Tolerates neglect**

Juice from the succulent leaves of this native of the Canary Islands is widely used to heal minor burns and soothe abrasions. With fleshy, green leaves edged with small spines, aloe is not spectacular to look at, but it is widely grown, especially in kitchens, because of its healing sap. Breaking or cutting a leaf releases the clear, gel-like sap, which may be applied directly to the skin and is used in many lotions.

Grow in bright light but not direct sun. Pot in standard all-purpose houseplant soil, and keep the soil evenly moist all year. Fertilize monthly with 20-10-10 plant food. Propagate from offsets.

FOXTAIL FERN
Asparagus densiflorus 'Myersii'

- **Medium size**
- **Compact**
- **Easy to grow**

This South African native is compact, and growing upright, it looks neater than its better-known relative, the sprawling asparagus fern. Foxtail fern and asparagus fern are close cousins of the edible asparagus.

Attractive and easy to grow, foxtail fern likes dappled sunlight. Pot in all-purpose potting soil, and keep the soil somewhat moist all year. Feed every other month with 20-10-10 fertilizer. Occasionally pinch back stems to keep the plant bushy. Propagate by division.

Cast Iron Plant

Aspidistra elatior

- Handsome medium-size plant
- Tolerates low light
- Difficult to kill

Few respectable Victorian homes with plants were without a cast iron plant in the parlor. The plant grows slowly in a compact clump of elongated shining dark green leaves that may eventually reach 3 feet tall. Unattractive purple-brown flowers may appear at the base. The plant survives low light and doesn't require a lot of water. Originally from China, cast iron plant is depicted in ancient Chinese paintings.

Grow in moderate to low light; the newer variegated forms need somewhat brighter conditions. Plant in a large pot in standard all-purpose houseplant soil. Keep the soil evenly moist except in winter, when the plant rests, and when soil can be allowed to become somewhat dry. Feed monthly with 20-10-5 fertilizer. Propagate by division.

Good cultivars: 'Milky Way', 'Variegata', 'Variegata Exotica'

Bottle Plant, Ponytail Palm
Beaucarnea recurvata (aka Nolina recurvata)

- Large plant
- Unusual structure
- Tolerates cool temperatures

If you forget to water this Mexican native, it maintains itself. It can store water for months in its swollen stem. The bottle-shaped stem (also compared to the shape of an elephant's foot) is adorned with a cluster of long, narrow ribbonlike arching leaves sprouting from the top. Indoors the plant grows to about 4 feet tall. Outdoors in mild climates, it can reach 6 feet.

Grow bottle plant in dappled light, and plant it in standard all-purpose potting soil. Allow the soil to dry out between waterings. Feed twice a year with 20-10-10 fertilizer. Keep potbound for best growth. Propagate from offsets.

Lily Family and Relatives cont'd

Variegated Spider Plant
Chlorophytum comosum cultivar

- **Medium size**
- **Striped beauty**
- **Trailing habit**

The handsome trailing spider (or airplane) plant from South Africa has been a favorite houseplant for decades, and the variegated cultivar shown is also popular. Spider plants need little care. The arching slender leaves are striped creamy white and give an airy appearance. The plant sends out miniature plantlets, called runners, on trailing wiry stems. (See pages 78 and 83.)

Spider plant finds a home in many offices, apartments, and dormitory rooms because it can be neglected for days without suffering ill effects. Grow in a somewhat sunny location, and use all-purpose potting soil kept evenly moist. The plant grows best when potbound. Feed four times a year with 20-10-10 fertilizer. Propagate by rooting the small, pendant runners that emerge.

Ti Plant
Cordyline terminalis

- **Medium-size to large plant**
- **Handsome colorful leaves**
- **Fast grower**

This relative of the dracaena clan has handsome foliage. Stripes of maroon, green, purple and white make a stunning combination. Mature ti plants are the most striking and make a great corner accent in a cachepot.

Grow ti plant in a bright location in well-drained humusy soil that you should keep evenly moist. Keep this plant out of full sun to avoid burning the foliage. Feed quarterly with 10-20-10 fertilizer. Repot only when it is potbound; the plant dislikes disturbance. Propagate from stem cuttings.

DWARF PINEAPPLE DRACAENA
Dracaena deremensis 'Compacta'

- Medium size
- Attractive foliage
- Easy to grow

Aptly named, pineapple dracaena has shiny green leaves that resemble a pineapple top. One among the vast number of available houseplants in the genus *Dracaena*, this one grows to 20 inches. It differs from most dracaenas because its leaves grow in a tight pineapple shape, compared with the open growth habits of other dracaena.

Grow in bright light, in standard all-purpose houseplant soil kept evenly moist all year. Feed quarterly with 10-20-10 fertilizer. The plant grows well on its own, so you don't need to fuss over it. Start new plants by division.

RED WINE CORN PLANT
Dracaena fragrans 'Red Wine'

- Large plant
- Striking foliage
- Easy to grow

The erect, slightly arching leaves of the corn plant are broad and pointed. 'Red Wine' has interesting maroon and green leaves. Another popular cultivar, 'Massangeana' has one or more yellow stripes down the center. Hailing from Africa, corn plants can grow to 60 inches tall. As they grow, the woody stem elongates, creating a treelike effect. Corn plants are undemanding and long-lived.

Grow in a bright location, and use a standard all-purpose houseplant soil that drains readily. Feed monthly with 20-20-10 fertilizer. Occasionally wipe foliage with a damp cloth to remove dust. Repot in fresh soil every second year. Purchase new plants from suppliers.

Other good cultivars: 'General Pershing', 'Lindeni'

$\mathcal{L}$ily Family and Relatives cont'd

$\mathcal{R}$AINBOW DRACAENA
Dracaena marginata 'Tricolor'
  (aka *D. cincta* 'Tricolor')

- Medium-size to large plant
- Handsome foliage
- Grows slowly

When rainbow dracaena was introduced to the houseplant trade in the late 1980s, its tricolored foliage caused a sensation. The narrow, swordlike green leaves are striped creamy white and edged in red. As a bonus, this beauty survives neglect, and adds a sculptural effect to the indoor garden. Mature plants are available and can grow to 60 inches.

Grow in a bright location with some sun. Pot in standard all-purpose houseplant soil kept evenly moist. Feed monthly with 10-10-10 fertilizer. Propagate from cane cuttings or by air layering. See page 90 for air layering instructions.

$\mathcal{S}$POTTED OX TONGUE PLANT
Gasteria bicolor var. *liliputana*

- Small plant
- Desirable succulent
- Slow grower

This stemless rosette of succulent, tongue-like, spotted leaves is the smallest of the genus gasteria, growing only to about 6 inches tall. Native to South Africa, the plant makes a good table accent.

Spotted tongue plant grows easily in bright light and thrives in a potting mix of equal parts sharp sand and potting soil. Keep the soil just barely moist all year. Avoid splashing water on leaves; otherwise they will become blemished. Feed quarterly with 10-10-10 fertilizer. Start new plants from offsets.

Silver Squill

Ledebouria socialis (aka *Scilla socialis*, *S. violacea*)

* **Small plant**
* **Attractive foliage**
* **Easy to grow**

From South Africa, this compact 24-inch plant has small blue-violet flowers that appear periodically set off by succulent green leaves spotted with silver. Silver squill is available through mail-order nurseries, often still sold under its former genus name, *Scilla*.

Grow this plant in a bright location, and pot it in standard all-purpose houseplant soil. Keep the soil barely moist all year. Feed quarterly with 10-10-10 fertilizer. Start new plants by tuber division.

Spineless Yucca

Yucca elephantipes

* **Medium-size to large plant**
* **Good floor accent**
* **Tolerates low light**

Spineless yucca is somewhat compact as yuccas grow, topping out at about 48 inches indoors. With spineless sword-shaped green leaves on a thick trunk, the plant is a good green accent where most other houseplants fail because it tolerates low light.

Grow in moderate to bright light in standard all-purpose houseplant soil kept evenly—and barely—moist all year. Feed quarterly with 20-10-10 fertilizer. This plant is also available as a mature specimen growing to 60 inches. Propagate by division.

Mulberry Family (MORACEAE)

Weeping Fig, Banyan Tree
Ficus benjamina

- Large treelike plant
- Likes humid rooms
- Easy to grow

Weeping fig has been a favorite houseplant for decades. The plant can grow tall and looks like a small tree, but it generally stays at about 40 inches indoors. The leaves are shiny green, and the form of mature plants is canopylike. Weeping fig has a reputation for being touchy, because it drops a lot of leaves if it doesn't get enough humidity.

Grow weeping fig in a bright but not sunny location and a humusy well-drained soil. Feed quarterly with 10-20-10 fertilizer. Propagate by air layering.

Braided Fig
Ficus benjamina

- Unique medium-size to large plant
- Handsome room accent
- Slow grower

Some nurseries sell this fancier version of the standard weeping fig. Its trunk is braided to create a unique stem. Braided fig was a trendy houseplant and quite popular some decades back; it has begun reappearing at plant centers. This handsome plant grows to about 36 inches and has a leafy crown.

Grow braided fig in a bright, airy location in standard all-purpose houseplant soil kept evenly moist. Feed quarterly with 10-20-10 fertilizer. Repot only when necessary. Keep this plant and weeping fig out of drafts. Purchase new plants from suppliers.

Variegated Fig
Ficus benjamina 'Variegata'

- Medium-size to large treelike plant
- Fine variegated foliage
- Easy to grow

This popular cultivar offers a canopy of handsomely variegated pale yellow and green leaves. It has a lacy appearance and more charm than the standard weeping fig.

Grow in bright to moderate light, even though the plant also grows well in low light. Pot in standard all-purpose houseplant soil. Feed monthly with 10-20-10 fertilizer. This plant needs little attention. Start new plants from stem cuttings.

BURGUNDY RUBBER PLANT
Ficus elastica 'Burgundy'

- ❧ **Large plant**
- ❧ **Good color**
- ❧ **Easy to grow**

Rubber plants are bold, tropical, and treelike and have large, green, oval leaves. In their native Asia, rubber plants become sizable trees. When cut, they bleed a sticky white sap. In the home, rubber plant grows to 36 inches, making a strong vertical accent. There are numerous cultivars.

Grow in moderate light, in standard all-purpose houseplant soil kept evenly moist. Wipe the leaves with a damp cloth occasionally. Feed only in spring and summer with 20-10-10 fertilizer. Propagate by air layering.

Other good cultivars: 'Decora', 'Variegata', 'Doescheri'

VARIEGATED CREEPING FIG
Ficus pumila 'Variegata'

- ❧ **Small to medium-size plant**
- ❧ **Tiny-leaved beauty**
- ❧ **Easy to grow**

This diminutive, slow-growing vining member of the genus ficus has great charm. The variegated cultivar's small buttonlike green leaves are edged with yellow. To train the plant vertically, place a small trellis in the pot for it to climb. This is an easy plant to grow, and the variegated leaves make it a good addition to home gardens.

Grow variegated creeping fig in a very bright location. Keep this plant in a small pot; it does best when the roots are slightly crowded. Pot it in a well-drained all-purpose houseplant soil. Keep the soil somewhat dry all year. Feed quarterly with 10-10-10 fertilizer. Propagate from cuttings.

Orchids (ORCHIDACEAE)

 STEFAN ISLER ORCHID

✕ *Burrageara* 'Stefan Isler'

- **Medium size**
- **Colorful orange-red flowers**
- **Winter bloomer**

This fine hybrid is a cross between ✕ *Vuylstekeara* and *Oncidium*. Obtain from orchid suppliers. It grows to 24 inches tall, flowers freely, and blooms twice a year with good care.

Grow in bright light, in medium-grade fir bark kept evenly moist all year. Provide warmth. Nighttime temperatures should never drop below 55°F. Feed monthly with 10-30-20 fertilizer. Propagate by division.

 GUATEMALAN ORCHID

Cattleya guatemalensis (aka *C. deckeri*)

- **Medium size**
- **Stunning flowers**
- **Tolerates cool conditions**

This orchid from Guatemala bears a cluster of bright pink flowers in autumn, reaching a compact 30 inches. The plant grows easily. When "orchidmania" beset England during the 1860s, this species was a prized possession, and breeders have used it ever since then to produce hybrid Cattleyas of similar flower color.

Provide a bright, somewhat sunny location. Nighttime temperatures can drop to 55°F. Pot in medium-grade fir bark kept evenly moist all year. Feed quarterly with 20-30-10 fertilizer. Start new plants by division.

 CORSAGE FLOWER

Cattleya hybrid

- **Medium size**
- **Dramatic, long-lasting flowers**
- **Tolerates neglect**

Orchids bear colorful flowers that last for weeks. With thousands of *Cattleya* hybrids available, orchids have become America's favorite houseplant. The Cattleya flower is now available in all colors except black.

Grow in a bright but not sunny location, and pot in medium-grade fir bark. Provide even moisture, but allow the plant to rest for two months with little water. Feed monthly with a 20-30-20 plant food, except when resting. Propagate by division.

W ILDCAT ORCHID

× *Colmanara* 'Wildcat'

- ❧ **Medium size**
- ❧ **Fine yellow-brown-white flowers**
- ❧ **Available from orchid suppliers**

This excellent hybrid flowers freely in winter and grows to just 24 inches tall.

Provide a bright location. Grow in medium-grade fir bark, and keep well watered all year. Provide minimum nighttime temperatures of 55°F. Propagate by division.

J ILL KATALINCA ORCHID

Cymbidium 'Jill Katalinca'

- ❧ **Large vertical plant**
- ❧ **Handsome large flowers**
- ❧ **Needs attention**

From the genus *Cymbidium*, native to India and China, comes this spectacular 48-inch hybrid, bearing large colorful flowers profusely on tall scapes. It makes good cut flowers but needs careful attention.

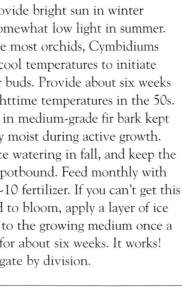

Provide bright sun in winter and somewhat low light in summer. Unlike most orchids, Cymbidiums need cool temperatures to initiate flower buds. Provide about six weeks of nighttime temperatures in the 50s. Grow in medium-grade fir bark kept evenly moist during active growth. Reduce watering in fall, and keep the plant potbound. Feed monthly with 10-20-10 fertilizer. If you can't get this orchid to bloom, apply a layer of ice cubes to the growing medium once a week for about six weeks. It works! Propagate by division.

S TARS 'N' BARS ORCHID

× *Degarmoara* 'Stars 'n' Bars'

- ❧ **Medium size**
- ❧ **Large, colorful, long-lasting flowers**
- ❧ **Easy to grow**

This hybrid is a robust grower with brown and yellow flowers in a bar pattern.

Provide bright light without direct sun. Plant in fine-grade fir bark kept evenly moist all year. Feed quarterly with 10-30-20 fertilizer, and don't fuss over the plant—it grows on its own. Propagate by division, or purchase new plants from suppliers.

Orchids cont'd

 ## Antelope Orchid
Dendrobium antennatum

- ❧ **Medium size**
- ❧ **Fine small white flowers**
- ❧ **Long-lasting blooms**

This pretty species from New Guinea was introduced in England in the mid-nineteenth century. There are several hybrids, two of which are shown here. Antelope orchid has erect stems to about 24 inches and small, fragrant flowers in a variety of colors. The flowers have twisted petals shaped like an antelope's horns. This orchid commands attention. In spring, it bears many flowers.

Provide bright light, and pot in medium-grade fir bark kept evenly moist. Average household temperatures suit this plant fine. Feed monthly with 10-20-10 fertilizer. Start new plants by division.

Topaz Dendrobium
Dendrobium bullenianum

- ❧ **Dependable medium-size plant**
- ❧ **Sometimes semideciduous**
- ❧ **Available from orchid suppliers**

A handsome orchid, not easy to find, but worth the search, this *Dendrobium* has stunning orange flowers borne in clusters from bare branches. The plant grows to 24 inches tall. Its sprawling stems become striking when the plant blooms in October.

Easy to grow, this orchid likes a bright, sunny location. Pot in fine-grade fir bark kept evenly moist all year. Feed quarterly with 20-30-20 fertilizer. Propagate by division.

 ## Epidendrum Stamfordianum
Epidendrum stamfordianum

- ❧ **Compact, medium-size plant**
- ❧ **Bears hundreds of tiny flowers**
- ❧ **Easy to grow**

Native to Central and South America, from Guatemala to Venezuela, this species bears a bountiful crop of small red-and-yellow flowers on graceful stems. A mature plant with hundreds of flowers makes quite an impression. A longtime favorite of hobbyists, this orchid will grow well without pampering.

Provide a bright location, and plant in medium-grade fir bark. Water thoroughly, but allow the medium to dry out between waterings. The plant tolerates nighttime temperatures as low as 55°F. Progagate new plants by division.

Dancing Lady Orchid
Oncidium maculatum 'Paolo'

- **Decorative medium-size plant**
- **Long-lasting fragrant flowers**
- **Easy to grow**

This orchid is a hybrid of *Oncidium maculatum*, which comes from Mexico and Central America and is a parent of many fine varieties. In nineteenth-century England, the species was prized. Here the original small-flowered species has been hybridized to create a plant with large flowers that bear the brown-and-yellow markings typical of Oncidiums. A pretty, compact plant, this one grows to 30 inches tall.

Provide this orchid with a bright, somewhat sunny location. Pot in medium-grade fir bark kept evenly moist all year. Keeping the plant in a small pot should force it to bloom. Feed quarterly with 20-10-10 fertilizer. Propagate by division.

Sharry Baby Orchid
Oncidium 'Sharry Baby'

- **Medium size**
- **Perfumed flowers**
- **Dependable bloomer**

This recently introduced orchid bears wands of highly scented flowers that last for weeks. Foliage is sometimes spotted red (not indicative of disease), and the plant grows to a compact 30 inches. It is easy to grow and blooms twice a year.

Grow this plant in a bright location in medium-grade fir bark kept moist all year. Feed quarterly with 20-30-10 fertilizer. Repot only when necessary—the plant dislikes disturbance. Propagate by division.

Lady Slipper Orchid
Paphiopedilum insigne

- **Medium size**
- **Decorative flowers**
- **Grows in low light**

Native to the Himalayas at elevations to 6,000 feet, this orchid not surprisingly tolerates cool temperatures and has been hybridized extensively because of its cold tolerance. The plant grows to 24 inches tall and bears green-brown-yellow pouch-like flowers, typical of lady slippers, on an erect stem. The blooms last for weeks.

Provide this plant with bright light, but no direct sun. Pot in fine-grade fir bark. Water evenly all year, and feed four times a year with 20-10-10 fertilizer. Propagate by division.

Orchids cont'd

RED SKY LADY SLIPPER ORCHID
Paphiopedilum 'Red Sky'

* Decorative small to medium-size plant
* Flowers last for weeks
* Easy to grow

This decorative hybrid orchid bears a lovely maroon-and-green flower on an erect stem with a distinctive maroon top. Its exotic appearance stunned British gardeners in the late 1800's. The leaves are mottled, and the plant is small, growing only to about 20 inches.

Provide a bright but not sunny location, and plant in fine-grade fir bark. Keep evenly moist, and feed twice a year with 20-10-5 fertilizer. Repot only when necessary. Propagate by division.

LADY SLIPPER ORCHID
Paphiopedilum sukhakulii

* Medium size
* Long-lasting exotic flowers
* Tolerates some coolness

This handsome orchid hails from Thailand and grows to 10 inches tall. Borne on erect stems, the single flowers are multicolored—spotted and banded in greens, browns, and tan. They appear in autumn or winter.

This orchid likes a warm location and moderate light. Plant in fine-grade fir bark kept evenly moist all year. Grow in a small pot to encourage bud formation. Feed monthly with 10-20-10 fertilizer. Propagate by division.

MOTH ORCHID, DOGWOOD ORCHID
Phalaenopsis hybrid

* Small plant
* Attractive foliage
* Blooms last a month or longer

There are thousands of hybrids of these wonderfully reliable orchids from Java, Southeast Asia, and the Philippines. The elegant arching wands of flowers are easy to coax into bloom. There are solid, striped, or spotted flowers in several colors. The nickname comes from the Greek *phalaina*, meaning moth, and aptly describes the shape of the blooms. Moth orchids also make good cut flowers.

Provide a bright location, in clay pots of medium-grade fir bark kept watered all year. Feed with 10-20-10 orchid fertilizer every third week. Repot in fresh fir bark every 18 months. Propagate from offsets that form around the base of the plant.

Moth Orchid

Phalaenopsis hybrid

- **Medium size**
- **Dozens of flowers**
- **Easy to grow**

Originally from the Philippines, this fine moth orchid bears plenty of flowers. It was introduced to the West in England about 1830. The flowers are small and yellow and appear in winter or spring. The plant grows to 24 inches tall with large oar-shaped leaves. Moth orchids are adaptable, resilient houseplants and a good choice for beginners.

Provide bright to moderate light and temperatures ranging from 55° to 80°F. Pot in medium-grade fir bark, and keep the medium moist but never soggy. Fertilize with 10-20-10 plant food every three months. Propagate from offsets.

Orange Cattleya

Sophrolaeliocattleya Hazel Boyd 'Sunset'

- **Medium size**
- **Long-lasting exquisite small flowers**
- **Easy to grow**

This beautiful orchid is a hybrid of three popular genera: *Sophronitis*, *Laelia*, and *Cattleya*. It bears lovely small orange and red flowers in typical cattleya form. Plants grow to 30 inches and bloom freely, sometimes twice a year.

Grow this plant in an airy, bright, somewhat sunny location. Plant in medium-grade fir bark kept evenly moist all year. Provide normal household temperatures. Feed quarterly with 20-30-10 fertilizer. Propagate by division.

Winter Orchid

Zygopetalum crinitum

- **Medium size**
- **Dramatic fragrant flowers**
- **Winter bloomer**

From tropical and South America, this handsome orchid has flowers that are a combination of brown and blue—and fragrant. Plus, they bloom in winter. The plant grows to 30 inches, with papery thin green leaves.

Grow winter orchid in a somewhat bright, cool area. Use medium-grade fir bark kept evenly moist most of the year. Feed monthly with 10-30-20 fertilizer, except during the month after flowering. Also decrease water then. Propagate by division.

$\mathcal{P}$alms (PALMAE)

$\mathcal{F}$ISHTAIL PALM
Caryota mitis

- Large tropical beauty
- Interesting, ragged-edge leaves
- Dark green fronds

Native to Southeast Asia, the popular fishtail palm is a decorative beauty that sometimes grows to 6 feet indoors. If you have the room, a well-grown plant is a beautiful sight, becoming lush and handsome as it matures. What's more, the fishtail palm can survive neglect and still look good. It needs vertical space.

Grow this plant in a bright but not sunny location. Pot in a large container with standard all-purpose houseplant soil kept evenly moist all year. Average household temperatures are fine. Repot it only when the roots grow from the bottom of the pot, and trim the leaves, which tend to turn brown at the edges. Feed this palm monthly with 20-20-10 fertilizer. Propagate from offsets or by division.

$\mathcal{B}$AMBOO PALM
Chamaedorea erumpens

- Large plant
- Best palm for home conditions
- Easy to grow

The Palm Family is large, but only a few species can tolerate home conditions. Bamboo palm does beautifully indoors, growing to 60 inches tall. Its canopy-type growth is especially attractive when used to fill in a corner. The plant's fronds are dense, and its stalks are stout.

Grow bamboo palm in a bright but not sunny place. Pot in standard all-purpose houseplant soil kept somewhat dry all year. This easy-to-grow palm adapts to both cool and warm household temperatures. Feed quarterly with 20-10-10 fertilizer. Propagate by division.

Butterfly Palm
Chrysalidocarpus lutescens

- Medium-size to large plant
- Graceful form
- Easy to grow

The fronds of this Madagascar native are slim and airy, and the plant has a fountainlike form. Butterfly palm grows to 40 inches and makes a good corner accent.

Provide a bright location. Grow in standard all-purpose potting soil kept evenly moist, never too dry or too wet. Feed quarterly with 20-20-10 fertilizer. Occasionally trim the bottom leaves, which can become straggly. Propagate by division.

Chinese Fan Palm
Licuala grandis

- Large, graceful plant
- Attractive in a decorative tub
- Easy to grow

When mature, this palm is a picture of grace. Its fan-shaped leaves are carried on tall stems. From New Guinea, the plant grows slowly to 48 inches tall.

Provide bright light without direct sun. Grow in a large decorative tub filled with humusy soil that drains readily. The plant tolerates cool evening temperatures as low as 55°F. Fertilize monthly with 10-10-10 plant food. Propagation is difficult under home conditions, so purchase new plants from suppliers.

Lady Palm
Rhapis excelsa

- Large plant
- Attractive mature specimen
- Easy to grow

This graceful plant may be the best potted palm. It bears fanlike fronds on tall canelike stems. Lady palm has often been depicted in paintings in its native China.

Grow lady palm in a large container with standard houseplant soil kept evenly moist all year. The plant tolerates moderate to low light. Feed with 20-20-10 fertilizer every three months. Repot lady palm every fourth year, and topdress it with fresh soil annually. Propagates easily from offsets.

Spiderwort Family (COMMELINACEAE)

*B*RAZILIAN WANDERING JEW
Callisia repens

- ❋ **Medium-size to large plant**
- ❋ **Small attractive leaves**
- ❋ **Easy to grow**

This plant is related to the tradescantias, which share the *wandering* common name. Attractive but overlooked, this dense trailing plant has small dark green leaves and is quite beautiful in a hanging basket. The stems can reach 48 inches long.

Grow in a hanging basket in bright to moderate light. Pot in standard all-purpose houseplant soil kept just moist, never soggy or dry. The plant likes good air circulation. Feed monthly with 10-10-5 fertilizer. Because this plant is difficult to propagate at home, you should purchase new plants from suppliers.

*M*OSES-IN-A-BOAT, MOSES-IN-THE-CRADLE
Rhoeo spathacea (aka *Tradescantia spathacea*)

- ❋ **Small to medium-size plant**
- ❋ **Tolerates low light**
- ❋ **Easy to grow**

This plant from Mexico gets its common name from the small white flowers tucked inside the boat-shaped bracts at the plant's base. The plant grows to about 20 inches tall, in a clump of stunning green and purple leaves. This is a popular plant because it is so easy to grow, has a compact shape, and tolerates low light. Indoor gardeners have grown this plant for decades.

Grow Moses-in-a-boat in bright to moderate light, without direct sun. Pot it in standard all-purpose houseplant soil kept evenly moist all year. Except for watering, the plant needs little attention to thrive. Feed quarterly with 10-10-10 fertilizer. Propagate by division or from stem or tip cuttings.

Purple Heart Plant
Setcreasea pallida (aka Tradescantia pallida)

- ✳ **Small accent plant**
- ✳ **Tufted leaves**
- ✳ **Easy to grow**

Though not a spectacular plant, purple heart is easy to grow and makes a pleasant small-table accent. The green leaves have purple undersides and grow in bunches along sprawling stems. Small pink flowers, as shown, may appear at stem tips in summer.

Grow purple heart plant in bright light to develop full coloration of the leaves. The plant can tolerate lower light, but then the foliage will be more green and less purple. Pot in a small container filled with humusy soil that drains readily. Keep the soil moderately moist all year, never too dry or too wet. Purple heart tolerates cool or warm household temperatures. Feed this plant quarterly with 10-10-10 fertilizer. Propagate from leaf or tip cuttings.

Wandering Jew
Zebrina pendula (aka Tradescantia zebrina)

- ✳ **Medium size**
- ✳ **Long-time favorite**
- ✳ **Fast-growing for hanging basket**

Numerous plants from Mexico and Central America share this common name. Some have greenish leaves; others have white-and-green striped foliage; and still others are striped with white, purple, and green. This species has green or purple leaves striped with creamy silver tops and purple undersides. It needs little attention to grow lush and vigorous.

Grow this plant in bright to moderate light, in standard all-purpose houseplant soil. Keep the soil evenly moist all year—the plant needs no rest period. Average household temperatures suit it fine. Trim stems when they start to get leggy. Feed every two weeks during active growth with 10-20-10 fertilizer. Propagate from cuttings.

Other Families

As explained on page 107 of the Plant Profiles, this subsection presents excellent houseplants from families that contain a much smaller portion of houseplants commercially available than the previous subsection does. As in the preceding profiles, here you'll find the plants arranged alphabetically by the family common name. Within each family, the plants are arranged alphabetically by the scientific name for the genus and species, which is a convention in gardening publications.

Reminder: There is another good reason for having two subsections in the Plant Profiles. It allows the grouping of plants from major families on whole pages and multiple two-page spreads on preceding pages, thereby helping you see the similarities and differences within families and genera (plural for genus).

In this subsection, you'll find anywhere from one to three representatives from each family. Whenever there is more than one plant represented from a given family, you'll find them on the same page or the same two-page spread for easy comparison.

Araucaria Family (ARAUCARIACEAE)

NORFOLK ISLAND PINE
Araucaria heterophylla (aka A. excelsa)

- **Treelike, large plant**
- **Needlelike green leaves**
- **Slow grower**

From Norfolk Island in the South Pacific, this plant grows tall outdoors but stays about 48 inches indoors. It has a handsome growth habit, with tiers of needle-covered branches, though it is not a pine.

Grow in bright light. Average household temperatures are fine. Plant in a large container, in standard all-purpose houseplant soil that drains readily. Keep soil evenly moist, but water sparingly in the winter. Mist occasionally. Feed quarterly with 20-10-10 fertilizer. The plant dislikes disturbance, so top-dress with fresh soil each year instead of repotting. Purchase new plants from suppliers rather than propagating.

Aucuba Family (AUCUBACEAE)

GOLD-DUST PLANT
Aucuba japonica

- **Compact medium size**
- **Handsome foliage plant**
- **Easy to grow**

From western Africa, the gold-dust dracaena is a compact, slow-growing foliage plant with green leaves dusted with golden yellow spots. These bushy plants grow to about 30 inches. Most of the numerous cultivars thrive in home conditions.

Grow in a bright airy location. Pot in standard all-purpose houseplant soil with excellent drainage. Keep the soil evenly moist all year, never too dry or too wet. Feed quarterly with 20-10-20 fertilizer. Propagate by division.

Banana Family (MUSACEAE)

Parrot Plant
Heliconia psittacorum

- Large vertical accent
- Beautiful orange-red flower bracts
- Handsome lance-shaped leaves

Heliconia is a large genus from Brazil in the same family as the banana plant. Plants called *Heliconia psittacorum* can lead to confusion because many different plants are listed with that scientific name. Several fine cultivars are available. Parrot plant has vertical stems sheathed with green leaves and tall spikes topped with exotic orange-red floral bracts that resemble those of the bird-of-paradise (*Strelitzia reginae*) but is a far more amenable houseplant. It grows to more than 48 inches and can be moved outdoors in summer.

Grow in a bright location, in a large pot of well-drained all-purpose houseplant soil. Keep the soil evenly moist all year. Heliconias thrive in warm conditions but will tolerate nighttime temperatures as low as 55°F. Feed monthly with 10-10-10 fertilizer. Propagate by division.

Bignonia Family (BIGONIACEAE)

China Doll Plant
Radermachera sinica

- Medium-size to large plant
- Attractive treelike shape
- Easy to grow

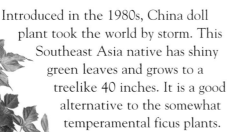

Introduced in the 1980s, China doll plant took the world by storm. This Southeast Asia native has shiny green leaves and grows to a treelike 40 inches. It is a good alternative to the somewhat temperamental ficus plants.

Grow in bright light, in standard all-purpose houseplant soil. Water sparingly all year. Feed monthly with 10-10-10 plant food. Propagate from tip cuttings.

Cycad Family (CYCADACEAE)

Sago Palm
Cycas revoluta

- Medium size
- Can grow to 36 inches across
- Survives neglect

This slow-growing Java native belongs to one of the oldest known plant families. It resembles a conifer and forms a trunk similar to a palm, and it needs little attention to thrive.

Sago palm needs bright light and standard all-purpose houseplant soil kept evenly moist all year. Repot only when necessary, about every third year. Purchase new plants from suppliers.

Dogbane Family (APOCYNACEAE)

Dipladenia
Mandevilla × amabilis

- ✤ **Excellent large basket plant**
- ✤ **Stunning large flowers**
- ✤ **Easy to grow**

Hailing from Brazil and formerly in the genus *Dipladenia*, this stellar plant bears large cerise flowers with yellow throats almost year-round. The plant is vining and can grow fast to 48 inches. Flowers are borne on fresh growth, so occasional pruning stimulates blooms.

Grow in bright light. Pot in a large container of standard all-purpose houseplant soil. Feed monthly with 20-10-10 fertilizer. In winter, let the soil dry out somewhat between waterings so that the plant can rest. Propagate from cuttings.

Good cultivar: 'Alice du Pont'

Gentian Family (GENTIANACEAE)

Persian Violet, German Violet
Exacum affine

- ✤ **Small plant**
- ✤ **Pretty purple flowers**
- ✤ **Easy to grow**

Growing to 14 inches, this bushy little plant has waxy leaves and small purple flowers with yellow centers. Although not spectacular, it makes a charming table accent. Or you can mass several for greater impact as a display for interiors. Persian violet is widely grown for gift-giving at holiday times. This plant has a lovely fragrance.

Grow in bright light, in well-drained all-purpose potting soil. Plant in a small pot, and keep the soil evenly moist all year. Do not fertilize. As the plant becomes straggly, take tip cuttings for new plants, and discard the old plant. (See Chapter 6, page 86 for instructions on taking tip cuttings.)

Geranium Family (GERANIACEAE)

Geranium
Pelargonium × hortorum

- ⚘ **Large plant with colorful flower heads**
- ⚘ **Favorite indoor and outdoor plant**
- ⚘ **Hundreds of varieties**

Blooming in shades of red, pink, and white, geraniums are tough to beat. But as permanent plants they are difficult to keep for more than a few months. The *Pelargonium × hortorum* hybrids, which most gardeners know as geraniums, are popular both as houseplants and as outdoor summer annuals. They are sometimes called zonal geraniums because the leaves of some cultivars are marked with dark, circular "zones."

Provide plenty of light and direct sun for best blooming. Plant in fast-draining all-purpose potting soil. Keep in small pots. In large pots, plants tend to get leggy and need pruning. A winter rest is needed, so water sparingly then. Feed monthly with 20-10-10 fertilizer, except during the winter rest. Propagate from stem cuttings.

Grape Family (VITACEAE)

Begonia Vine
Cissus discolor

- ⚘ **Small to medium-size plant**
- ⚘ **Handsome foliage**
- ⚘ **Easy to grow**

This beautiful vine has arrow-head-shaped leaves of silver, green, purple, and pink.

Grow in a bright but not sunny location, in humusy soil that drains readily. Keep the soil evenly moist all year—it's temperamental about watering. Feed monthly with 20-10-10 fertilizer. Pinch back leaves to encourage bushier growth. Propagate from stem cuttings.

Hydrangea Family (HYDRANGEACEAE)

Hydrangea
Hydrangea macrophylla

- ⚘ **Bountiful flowers**
- ⚘ **Medium-size gift plant**
- ⚘ **Excellent temporary decoration**

Hydrangea features large round flower clusters 8 to 10 inches in diameter. Cultivars have flowers that last six weeks in pink, blue, red, or white. Purchase hydrangeas in spring or summer—the normal blooming season.

This plant likes bright light and evenly moist soil. If too dry, the plant quickly dies. Do not fertilize. Start new plants from stem cutting.

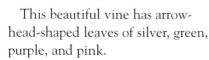

*M*adder Family (RUBIACEAE)

*C*APE *J*ASMINE
Gardenia jasminoides (aka G. augusta)

- Compact medium-size plant
- Fragrant flowers
- Attractive foliage

This plant is a native of China. Although difficult to grow, it is a favorite with hobbyists because its creamy white flowers can deliciously scent an entire room.

Cape jasmine and its cultivar 'Radicans' need time to adjust to new surroundings when you bring them home. Provide a location in bright light without direct sun. To avoid bud drop—the most common gardenia problem—avoid drastic temperature changes. Also, provide more humidity during the winter. Keep the soil evenly moist, and feed monthly with an acidic fertilizer. Gardenias are difficult to propagate at home. Instead, purchase new plants.

*E*GYPTIAN *S*TAR *C*LUSTER
Pentas lanceolata

- Good medium-size plant
- Colorful flowers
- Many cultivars

Native to Africa, these plants grow to 36 inches and have clusters of star-shaped flowers in spring through summer. The flowers can be yellow, pink, red, or orange.

Grow in a sunny location, in sandy soil. Keep the soil evenly moist all year. If the soil dries out, the leaves will drop, but avoid overly wet soil as well. Feed monthly with 20-10-10 fertilizer. Propagate by division.

*M*allow Family (MALVACEAE)

*F*LOWERING *M*APLE
Abutilon × hybridum

- Pretty bell-shaped flowers
- Large vertical plant
- Difficult to grow

This plant has maplelike leaves variegated with white in some cultivars. A favorite houseplant for over 100 years, flowering maple has been much hybridized and can grow to 48 inches. The lovely bell-shaped flowers come in shades of red, rose, orange, pink, and yellow. The plant wilts quickly without proper watering.

Grow in a sunny spot, and use a houseplant soil that drains readily. The plant must never be dry or too wet. In hot weather it may need watering every other day. Do not fertilize. Provide warm temperatures, and cut back the stems occasionally. Propagate from cuttings.

Prayer Plant

Calathea majestica 'Roseolineata'
(aka *C. ornata* 'Roseolineata')

 Medium size
Beautifully marked leaves
Easy to grow

The leaves close at night like hands folded in prayer. This pretty cultivar grows to 28 inches tall.

Grow in bright light, in humusy soil that drains readily. Keep the soil evenly moist all year; allow it to dry somewhat in the winter. The plant needs average household temperatures. Feed quarterly with 10-10-10 fertilizer. Propagate by division.

Peacock Plant

Calathea makoyana

Excellent medium-size plant
Colorful foliage
Easy to grow

This Brazilian native grows to a compact 24 inches. The many cultivars are often confused with the related prayer plants.

Peacock plants like a bright but not sunny window, but they don't respond well to drafts or temperature changes. Use a standard all-purpose houseplant soil kept evenly moist. If plants receive too much or too little moisture, they will not thrive. Mist the leaves regularly. Repot every year, and feed monthly with 20-20-10 fertilizer. Propagate by division.

Melastoma Family (MELASTOMACEAE)

Pink Grape Plant

Medinilla magnifica

Large, handsome plant
Pendant flower heads
Easy to grow

This plant bears large, drooping clusters of pink flowers and bracts, followed by long-lasting purple berries. Another species, M. *myriantha*, is similar in appearance but somewhat smaller and with pink berrylike flowers. This tropical shrub grows to some 48 inches and sports, thick-veined green leaves and pendant flower scapes in summer.

Grow in bright light. Use a humusy potting soil kept quite moist in warm months, somewhat drier the rest of the year. Provide high humidity. Feed twice a month with 10-20-10 fertilizer. Because the plant dislikes disturbance, repot it only when necessary—about every second year. Propagate by division.

Milkweed Family (ASCLEPIADACEAE)

MADAGASCAR JASMINE
Stephanotis floribunda

- Large plant
- Intensely fragrant flowers
- Vining growth habit

In the summer months, this vining Madagascar jasmine responds well to cool conditions and bears a profusion of highly scented waxy white flowers that brighten any indoor garden. The flowers are often used in bridal bouquets.

Grow in a bright but not sunny location. Pot in standard all-purpose houseplant soil, and provide a support for the vining stems. Feed monthly with 20-10-10 fertilizer. Keep the soil evenly moist for most of the year. In winter decrease watering somewhat, but never allow the soil to become dry enough to cake. Madagascar jasmine needs nighttime temperatures of 55°F to set buds. Propagate from runners.

Mint Family (LABIATAE)

PAINTED NETTLE
Coleus blumei (aka Solenostemon scutellarioides)

- Fast-growing small plant
- Colorful foliage
- Easy to grow

Coleus is often planted as an outdoor annual in shady gardens, but it also grows well indoors. The foliage is colorful, and there are some 200 different hybrids with leaves of varying shapes and sizes in many combinations of colors. The plants are generally good for only a season, but tip cuttings root easily to create new plants.

Coleus likes bright light and a humusy, well-drained potting soil. Keep the soil evenly moist, neither too dry nor too wet. Feed every few weeks with 10-20-10 fertilizer. Pinch off flowers to keep the foliage in better condition. Tip cuttings root easily in water or soil.

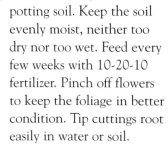

SWEDISH IVY
Plectranthus australis

- Medium size
- Handsome trailer for a hanging basket
- Easy to grow

This old-time favorite, with dense green, scalloped leaves, needs little care to thrive.

Provide bright to moderate light, ideally with a bit of morning sun. Pot in standard all-purpose houseplant soil. Keep the soil evenly moist except in winter. But never allow the soil to become dry. Feed quarterly with 10-10-10 fertilizer. Wipe the leaves occasionally with a damp cloth. Prune when needed to control shape—the plant can grow quickly. Propagate from stem cuttings.

Pepper Family (PIPERACEAE)

TRAILING PEPEROMIA
Peperomia obtusifolia

- Medium size
- Attractive foliage
- Sturdy trailer

From the jungles of Mexico and northern South America, trailing peromia comes in many varieties. Grow in bright light, and plant in all-purpose houseplant soil. Too much water causes problems and too little stunts growth, so keep the soil evenly moist. Propagate by division or by taking cuttings.

COMMON PEPEROMIA
Peperomia scandens

- Medium size
- Old-time favorite
- Easy to grow

This bushy, somewhat sprawling plant can become large, and it grows quickly to 36 inches. The attractive oblong, succulent leaves come in variegated as well as plain green forms. Common peperomia needs little care to thrive.

Grow in bright light, and plant in standard all-purpose houseplant soil. Keep the soil evenly moist all year. Feed monthly with 10-10-10 fertilizer. Start new plants from tip cuttings.

Primrose Family (PRIMULACEAE)

FLORIST'S CYCLAMEN, SHOOTING STAR
Cyclamen persicum

- Colorful flowers
- Small seasonal plant
- Innumerable hybrids, including miniatures

Growing to a compact 24 inches, these free-flowering plants with decorative foliage generally bloom in fall and winter. Cyclamens grow from a tuber and are usually gift plants used as table accents that are discarded after blooming.

Grow in bright light, and plant in standard all-purpose houseplant soil. Keep the soil evenly moist—never let it dry out. No fertilization is necessary. Purchase new plants rather than attempting propagation.

Rose Family (ROSACEAE)

 ## Miniature Rose
Rosa chinensis 'Minima'

- Small cousin of garden roses
- Range of flower colors
- Seasonal plant

Miniature roses are diminutive versions of their larger outdoor cousins. Of the hundreds of hybrids, most are derived from *Rosa chinensis*. The plants usually grow about 14 inches tall.

Give miniature roses bright light and standard all-purpose houseplant soil. Keep the soil evenly moist. It is not necessary to fertilize the plants, because they are usually discarded after blooming. Purchase new plants from suppliers.

Sunflower Family (COMPOSITAE)

 ## Wax Vine
Senecio macroglossus

- Medium size
- Unusual ivy-type vine
- Easy to grow

A vigorous plant with fleshy leaves more pointed than those of English ivy, the wax vine is handsome and needs little attention to thrive.

Grow in bright light, in standard houseplant soil. Keep the soil evenly moist except in winter, when you can leave the soil barely moist. Feed monthly with 20-10-10 fertilizer. Propagate from cuttings.

Saxifrage Family (SAXIFRAGACEAE)

 ## Strawberry Begonia
Saxifraga stolonifera (aka *S. sarmentosa*)

- Small trailing plant
- Grows well indoors
- Easy to grow

This native to Japan and China is neither a strawberry nor a begonia. The common name derives from the runners that trail from the plant, similar to those on a strawberry plant, and the leaves, which have the same general shape as those of some begonias. This plant grows about 14 inches high, with white veined leaves.

Grow in bright to moderate light. Pot in standard all-purpose houseplant soil kept evenly moist all year. Feed every month with 10-10-10 fertilizer. Propagate from runners.

GLOSSARY

Air layering. A propagation method for plants with woody stems. See page 90.

Amendments. Organic or mineral materials, such as peat moss, compost, or vermiculite, used to improve soil.

Axil. The angle at which a leaf joins a stem.

Bract. A modified leaf or leaflike structure that often embraces a flower bud and opens with the flower. Bracts occur at the base of the flower stem and may be part of the flower head. Usually small and green, some bracts, such as those of poinsettia, are mistaken for flower petals.

Bud. A protrusion on a plant stem that develops into a flower.

Bulb. A fleshy underground structure from which a flowering plant develops. The term *bulb* is often used loosely to refer to corms, rhizomes, and tubers, as well as true bulbs.

Cachepot. A decorative plant container without drainage holes.

Come true. When an offspring plant grows to be identical to its parent, it is said to *come true*. The only way to ensure that a hybrid plant comes true is to vegetatively propagate it, such as by cuttings or division.

Corm. A fleshy underground structure from which a flowering plant grows. Curcuma grows from a corm. See *Bulb*.

Cotyledon (pronounced *cot-l-EED-n*). The first leaf or pair of leaves a seedling sprouts; also called *seed leaves* (usually round or oval).

Crown. The junction of roots and stem, usually at soil level. See page 66.

Cultivar. Short for *culti*-vated *var*-iety. A plant variety developed in cultivation, rather than occurring in nature.

Culture. General plant care. Good culture results in optimal growing conditions.

Cutting. A plant part (usually a stem or leaf section) removed and rooted to grow a new plant.

Damping-off. A fungal disease that attacks seedlings and causes them to collapse.

Daylength. The number of hours of daylight that a plant receives in a 24-hour period.

Day-neutral plants. Plants that do not require a particular daylength and will flower at various times of the year. See *Daylength*.

Division. A propagation method that separates a plant into two or more similar pieces, each with at least one bud and some roots.

Epiphyte. A plant that is not rooted in soil. Epiphytes grow on other plants and obtain their nourishment and moisture from the air.

Exposure. The intensity and duration of light a plant receives.

Fir bark. A potting medium in which orchids and bromeliads are often planted.

Forcing. Causing a plant to flower indoors ahead of its natural blooming time.

Genus (plural: genera). A closely related group of species sharing similar characteristics and probably evolved from the same ancestors.

Germination. The sprouting of a seed.

Habit. The characteristic shape, or form, a plant assumes as it grows.

Horticultural charcoal. A clean by-product of burned wood. Applied to plant wounds, it decreases the chances of diseases starting there. Also used to keep water fresh.

Humus. The fibrous residues of decomposed organic materials in soil. Humus provides nutrients and helps the potting medium drain.

Hybrid. A plant resulting from cross-breeding of parents that belong to different varieties, species, or genera. Seeds of hybrids often do not come true but revert to the traits of one of the parent plants. See *Come true*.

Leaf cutting. A propagation method that stimulates cut pieces of leaves to grow roots.

Leggy. Weak, elongated growth, usually caused by insufficient light.

Long-day plants. Plants that require long days to set buds, meaning that they bloom in summer, when days are long.

Mist. To spray a plant with water droplets. This cleans foliage and adds humidity to the plant's environment.

Native. A plant that occurs naturally in a particular geographic region.

Node. The point along a stem from which a leaf or roots emerge.

Offset. A new plant that forms at the base of the parent plant. Most bromeliads reproduce from offsets.

Peat moss. Partially decomposed mosses and sedges mined from boggy areas and used to improve the texture of a soil.

Perlite. Heat-expanded volcanic glass used to lighten potting mediums and create space for air particles.

Photoperiod. See *Daylength*.

Potbound. A plant with a root mass that has grown too large for its container. The overgrown roots take on the shape of the vessel, grow in circles, and may strangle the plant.

Potting medium. The material in which a plant is potted.

Potting mix. A blend of growing mediums for container-grown plants.

Propagate. To biologically reproduce plants.

(Continued on next page)

Pseudobulb. A swollen organ through which orchids reproduce.

Repotting. Transplanting from one container to another, usually to a larger container.

Resting period. The time when a plant's growth naturally slows, often after flowering.

Rhizome. A horizontal underground stem from which a new plant can grow. See *Bulb*.

Rooting hormone. A liquid or powder that encourages cuttings to root.

Rootball. A plant's combined mass of roots and soil.

Rosette. Foliage emerging from a central cluster.

Runners. A slender arching or trailing shoot that emerges from a mature plant. New plantlets form along the nodes of the shoot.

Scape. The flower stalk arising from the center of a plant.

Seed leaves. See *Cotyledon*.

Seed pellet. An organic, manufactured disk that expands when watered to become a seed container.

Seedling. A tiny new plant that has grown from seed.

Shards. Broken crockery used in the bottom of pots to aid in drainage.

Sharp sand. A coarse sand used as a potting medium and often sold as builder's sand.

Short-day plants. Plants that will not bloom unless they receive enough hours of darkness each day.

Sow. To spread and plant seeds.

Spadix. A flower spike protected by a spathe. See *Spathe* below and photo on page 125.

Spathe. A leaflike hood protecting the spadix. The peace lily flower is surrounded by a spathe. See page 125.

Species. A group of plants that shares many characteristics and can interbreed freely.

Specimen plant. A large plant often displayed on its own or in a prominent position.

Spike. An elongated flower cluster, with individual flowers borne on short stalks or attached directly to the main stem. See page 135.

Standard houseplant soil. A commercially available blend that provides ample drainage and air yet doesn't dry out quickly.

Stem cutting. A propagation method that stimulates root growth from the cut end of a stem.

Sterile medium. A soilless mix used for germinating seeds and rooting cuttings.

Stolon. A stem that produces a new plant at its tip.

Succulent. A plant with fleshy, thick foliage that retains moisture.

Tip cutting. A propagation method that employs the cut tips of leaves to start root growth.

Transplanting. The process of replanting a plant in new soil.

True leaves. The second pair of leaves that emerge on a seedling. These leaves have the distinctive shape of leaves of the mature plant.

Tuber. A fleshy underground structure from which plants emerge. See *Bulb*.

Urn. A water-holding, vase-like shape formed by leaves in bromeliads; also called a *vase*.

Variegated. Foliage that is marked, striped, or blotched with a color or colors other than green.

Variety. A variant of a species that is the result of natural mutation.

Vegetative propagation. Producing new plants from parts of a parent. The resulting plants are genetically identical to the parent plant.

Vermiculite. A mica product used in potting mixes. It retains water and releases it as the surrounding soil dries.

Metric Equivalents

All measurements in this book are given in U.S. Customary units. To find metric equivalents, use the following tables and conversion factors.

Inches to cm *(1 in = 2.54cm)*

in.	cm
7/64	0.2778
1/8	0.3175
1/4	0.6350
3/8	0.9525
1/2	1.2700
5/8	1.5875
3/4	1.9050
1	2.5400

Inches to cm *(1 in = 2.54cm)*

in.	cm
1	2.54
5	12.70
10	25.40

Feet to meters *(1 ft = 0.3048m)*

ft.	m
1	0.3048
5	1.5240
10	3.0480

Square feet to square meters
1 ft² = 0.092 903 04m²

Ounces/pounds (Avoirdupois) to g
1 oz. = 28.349 523g
1 lb. = 453.5924g

Pounds to kilograms
1 lb. = 0.453 592 37kg

Ounces/quarts to liters
1 oz. = 0.029 573 53L
1 qt. = 0.9463L

Gallons to liters
1 gal. = 3.7852L

Fahrenheit to c *(°C = °F − 32 × 5/9)*

°F	°C
50	10.00
60	15.56
70	21.11
80	26.67

INDEX

Note: Numbers in bold type indicate pages with photos or illustrations of the subject.

A

Abutilon × *hybridum* (flowering maple), **180**
Acalypha hispida (chenille plant), **147**
Acanthus family (Acanthaceae), 12, **108–111**
Adenium obesum (desert rose), **140**
Adiantum tenerum (lacy maidenhair fern), **148**
Aechmea
    chantinii hybrid (silver urn plant), **132**
    fasciata (urn plant), **132**
Aeschynanthus species (lipstick plant), **152**
African violet (*Saintpaulia* cultivars), **153**
Aglaonema (Chinese evergreen)
    'Amelia', **116**
    'Camilla', **116**
Alcohol, rubbing, to kill aphids, 101
Alocasia
    × *amazonica* (shield plant), **116**
    'Black Velvet', **117**
    cuprea (copper alocasia), **117**
    'Green Goddess', **118**
Aloe
    bellatula (aloe), **158**
    vera, aka *A. barbadensis* (healing aloe, medicine plant), **14**, **158**
Amaryllis (*Hippeastrum* cultivars), **113**
Amaryllis family (Amaryllidaceae), 16, **112–113**
Amazon lily (*Eucharis* × *grandiflora*), 12, **112**
Ananas cosmosus 'Variegatus' (variegated pineapple plant), **133**
Angel's wings (*Xanthosoma lindenii*, aka *Caladium lindenii*), **126**
Anthurium
    hookeri (tailflower), **118**
    scherzerianum and *A. andraeanum* (flamingo flower), **119**
Ants, **98**
Aphelandra squarrosa (zebra plant, yellow plume plant), **108**
Aphids, identifying, 98; killing, 101
Aralia family (Araliaceae), 12, **114–115**
    Balfour (*Polyscias scutellaria* 'Balfourii') **115**
    finger (*Dizygotheca elegantissima*), **114**
    false, *see Dizygotheca elegantissima*
    ming (*Polyscias fruticosa*), **114**
Araucaria excelsa, see Araucaria heterophylla
Araucaria family (Araucariaceae), **176**
Araucaria heterophylla, aka *A. excelsa* (Norfolk Island pine), **176**
Aroid family (Araceae), 13, **116–127**
Arrowhead plant (*Syngonium podophyllum*), **126**

Asparagus densiflorus 'Myersii' (foxtail fern), **158**
Aspidistra elatior (cast iron plant), **159**
Asplenium nidus (bird's nest fern), **148**
Aucuba family (Aucubaceae); gold-dust plant (*Aucuba japonica*), **176**

B

Banana family (Musaceae), **177**
Banyan tree, *see* weeping fig
Beaucarnea recurvata, aka *Nolina recurvata* (bottle plant, ponytail palm), **159**
Begonia
    angel-wing, **130**
    'Cleopatra', **128**
    × *hiemalis* (Reiger begonia), **128**
    'Kewensis', **129**
    'Picotee', **130**
    red-leaf, **129**
    Rex-Cultorum hybrid (rex), **130**
    Semperflorens-Cultorum hybrid (wax), **131**
    superba 'Rana' (maple-leaf), **131**
Begonia family (Begoniaceae), 16–17, **128–131**
Begonia vine (*Cissus discolor*), **179**
Beloperone guttata, see Justicia brandegeana
Bignonia family (Bigoniaceae), **177**
Billbergia 'Fantasia' (Fantasia bromeliad), **133**
Blechnum gibbum (tree fern), **149**
Botrytis blight, 103
Bottle plant (*Beaucarnea recurvata*), **159**
Bromeliad family (Bromeliaceae), 17, **132–139**
    blushing (*Neoregelia* hybrid), **137**
    Fantasia (*Billbergia* 'Fantasia'), **133**
    plume (*Tillandsia cyanea*), **137**
    tufted (*Tillandsia ionantha*), **138**
Bulbs
    forcing for winter color, 92–93
    propagating, 91
    tips for forcing, 93
Buying plants, 40

C

Cacti and succulents, 18, **140–146**
Cactus
    ball (*Parodia penicillata*), **144**
    Christmas (*Schlumbergera* × *buckleyi*), **145**
    Easter (*Rhipsalidopsis rosea*), 18, **144**
    globe (*Mamillaria celsiana*), **143**
    peanut (*Chamaecereus sylvestrii*), **140**
    pencil (*Rhipsalis* species), **144**
    Thanksgiving (*Schlumbergera truncata*), **145**
    torch (*Trichocereus candicans*), 18, **146**

Caladium × *hortulanum*, aka *C. bicolor*, **119**
Caladium lindenii, see Xanthosoma lindenii
Calathea
    majestica 'Roseolineata', aka *C. ornata* 'Roseolineata' (prayer plant), **181**
    makoyana (peacock plant), **181**
Calla lily, **20**
    golden calla lily (*Zantedeschia elliottiana*), **127**
Callisia repens (Brazilian wandering Jew), **174**
Camille dumbcane, *see* Dumbcane (*Dieffenbachia*)
Cape jasmine (*Gardenia jasminoides*), **20**, **180**
Cape primrose (*Streptocarpus* hybrid), **155**
Care
    air circulation, 70
    bringing plants indoors, 75–76
    fertilizer, 70–71
    heat and humidity, 69–70
    light, 58–59
    potting, 65
    potting mediums, 64
    repotting, 66 67
    seasonal and vacation, 74–77
    soil, 64
    taking plants outdoors, 75
    trimming and grooming, 72–73
    watering, 68
Caryota mitis (fishtail palm), **172**
Cast iron plant (*Aspidistra elatior*), **159**
Catherine wheel, *see Haemanthus katherinae*
Chamaecereus sylvestrii, aka *Echinopsis chamaecereus* (peanut cactus), **140**
Chamaedorea erumpens (bamboo palm), **172**
Chenille plant (*Acalypha hispida*), **147**
    as hanging plant, 51
China doll plant (*Radermachera sinica*), **177**
Chinese evergreen (*Aglaonema*)
    'Amelia', **116**
    'Camilla', **116**
    decorating in masses, 27
Chlorophytum comosum cultivar (variegated spider plant), **160**
Christmas cactus (*Schlumbergera* × *buckleyi*), **145**
Chrysalidocarpus lutescens (butterfly palm), **173**
Chrysanthemum, as gift, **20**
Cissus discolor (begonia vine), **179**
Clivia miniata (kaffir lily), **112**
Codiaeum variegatum var. *pictum* (croton), **147**
Coleus blumei, aka *Solenostemon scutellarioides* (painted nettle), **182**
Colocasia 'Hilo Beauty', aka *Alocasia* 'Hilo Beauty', **120**
Color, as accent for rooms, 28–30
    color wheel, leaf and petal, 29

Columnea arguta (button columnea), **152**
Containers
  boxes, 54
  choosing, 54–55
  decorating with, 26
  hanging, 50–51
  hardware for hanging, 51
  list of hanging plants for, 51
  recycled, for propagating, 79
  tubs and urns, 54
  see also Hanging plants, Pots
Cordyline terminalis (ti plant), **160**
Corn plant
  (*Dracaena fragrans* 'Red Wine'), **161**
Costus
  curvibracteatus (orange tulip), **156**
  cuspidatus (crepe paper flower), **156**
Crassula argentea, *see Crassula ovata*
Crassula ovata,
  aka *Crassula argentea* (jade tree), **140**
Creeping fig (*Ficus pumila*)
  as fine-textured plant, 28,
  'Variegata', **165**
Crepe paper flower (*Costus cuspidatus*,
  aka *C. igneus*), **19**, **156**
Crossandra infundibuliformis
  (firecracker flower), **108**
Croton (*Codiaeum variegatum* var. *pictum*),
  147
Crown-of-thorns (*Euphorbia milii*), **16**, **141**
Cryptanthus species and hybrids
  (earth star), **134**
Curcuma
  alismatifolia (Siam tulip), **156**
  species (Java tulip), **157**
Cuttings
  leaf, **87**
  leaf-section, **88**
  propagating, 86–87
  tip, **86**
  whole-leaf, **89**
Cycad family (Cycadaceae), **177**
Cycas revoluta (sago palm), **177**
Cyclamen persicum
  (florist's cyclamen, shooting star), **183**
Cyrtomium falcatum (holly fern), **149**

D
Decorating with plants, 22–32
  color, 28–30
  color wheel, leaf and petal, **29**
  containers, 26, 50–57
  displaying, 24–25
  elements of design, 25–30
  form (shape), 26
  light, artificial and sunlight, 28–29
  lighting, accent, flood-, spot-, track, 33
  mass (group of forms), 27
  matching plants to rooms, 31–32
  nongreen plants, 30
  pedestals, 55
  placement, 31–33

scale, 28
techniques, 23–24
texture, 28
Desert rose (*Adenium obesum*), **140**
Design elements, 25–30
Dieffenbachia (dumbcane)
  picta 'Camille', **120**
  picta 'Exotica', **121**
  'Tropic Snow', **121**
Dipladenia (*Mandevilla* × *amabilis*), **178**
Diseases
  botrytis blight, 103
  fungal, 102–103
  powdery mildew, 103
  preventive measures, 103
Displaying plants for room decor, 24–25
Dividing
  African violets, 85
  bromeliads, 85
  most plants, 84
  orchids, 85
Dizygotheca elegantissima
  (finger aralia), **114**
Dogbane family (Apocynaceae), **178**
Donkey's tail (*Sedum morganianum*), **146**
Dracaena
  cincta 'Tricolor', *see D. marginata* 'Tricolor'
  deremensis 'Compacta'
    (dwarf pineapple dracaena), **161**
  fragrans 'Red Wine'
    (Red Wine corn plant), **161**
  marginata 'Tricolor'
    (rainbow dracaena), **162**
Dryopteris erythrosora
  (Japanese shield fern), **149**
Dumbcane (*Dieffenbachia*)
  Camille (*D. picta* 'Camille'), **13**, **120**
  Exotica (*D. picta* 'Exotica'), **121**
  Tropic Snow (*D.* 'Tropic Snow'), **121**
Dwarf pineapple dracaena
  (*Dracaena deremensis* 'Compacta'), **161**

E
Earth star
  (*Cryptanthus* species and hybrids), **134**
Easter lily (*Lilium longiflorum*), **20**
Echeveria hybrid (false rose), **141**
Echinocereus candicans,
  see Trichocereus candicans
Echinopsis chamaecereus,
  see Chamaecereus sylvestrii
Egyptian star cluster (*Pentas lanceolata*), **180**
Emerald Gem homalomena (*Homalomena
rubescens* 'Emerald Gem'), **122**
Epipremnum
  aureum 'Marble Queen'
    (Marble Queen pothos), **121**
  'Satin' (Satin pothos), **122**
Episcia cupreata (flame violet), **152**
Eucharis × *grandiflora* (Amazon lily), **112**
Euphorbia family (Euphorbiaceae), **18**, **147**
  crown-of-thorns (*Euphorbia milii*), **141**

poinsettia (*Euphorbia pulcherrima*), **147**
Exacum affine (Persian violet,
  German violet), **178**

F
False rose (*Echeveria* hybrid), **141**
Fancy-leaved caladium (*Caladium
  × hortulanum*, aka *C. bicolor*), **119**
Felt bush (*Kalanchoe beharensis*), **142**
Ferns, 13, **148–151**
  decorating in masses, 27
  for hanging, 51
  bird's nest (*Asplenium nidus*), **148**
  button (*Pellaea rotundifolia*), **150**
  cabbage head (*Polypodium vulgare*), **13**, **151**
  Cretan brake (*Pteris cretica*), **151**
  holly (*Cyrtomium falcatum*), **149**
  Japanese shield
    (*Dryopteris erythrosora*), **13**, **149**
  lacy maidenhair (*Adiantum tenerum*), **148**
  leather (*Rumohra adiantiformis*), **151**
  tree (*Blechnum gibbum*), **149**
Fertilizer
  natural, 70–71
  spikes, **71**
  rules for feeding, 71
  synthetic, 71
Ficus
  benjamina (weeping fig, banyan tree,
    braided fig), **164**
  benjamina 'Variegata' (variegated fig), **164**
  elastica 'Burgundy'
    (burgundy rubber plant), **165**
  pumila 'Variegata'
    (variegated creeping fig), **165**
Fig, *see Ficus*
Fingernail plant (*Neoregelia spectabilis*), **137**
Fireball (*Haemanthus katherinae*), **113**
Firecracker flower
  (*Crossandra infundibuliformis*), **108**
Fittonia verschaffeltii (mosaic plant), **109**
Flaming sword (*Vriesea splendens*), **139**
Flamingo flower
  (*Anthurium scherzerianum*,
    and *A. andraeanum*), **119**
Floodlights, as room accent, 33
Florist's cyclamen
  (*Cyclamen persicum*), **183**
  as gift, 20
Flowering maple (*Abutilon* × *hybridum*), **180**
Flowering plants, 16–19
Fluffy Ruffles Boston fern
  (*Nephrolepis exaltata* 'Fluffy Ruffles'), **150**
Foliage plants, 11–15
Forcing bulbs
  tips, 93
  for winter color, 92–93
Foxtail fern (*Asparagus densiflorus* 'Myersii'),
  158
Fungal diseases, 102–103

G

Gardenia augusta, see G. jasminoides
Gardenia jasminoides,
    aka G. augusta (Cape jasmine), **180**
Gasteria bicolor var. liliputana
    (spotted ox tongue plant), **162**
Gentian family (Gentianaceae), **178**
Geranium (Pelargonium × hortorum), **179**
Geranium family (Geraniaceae), **179**
German violet, see Persian violet
Germinating seeds, **81**
Gesneriad family (Gesneriaceae),
    18–19, **152–155**
Gift plants, 20
Ginger family (Zingiberaceae), 19, **156–157**
    White Dragon butterfly ginger
        (Globba winitti 'White Dragon'), **157**
Gloxinia (Sinningia hybrid), 18, **154**
Gold-dust plant (Aucuba japonica), **176**
Goldfish plant (Nematanthus gregarius), **153**
    for hanging, 21, 51
Grape family (Vitaceae), **179**
Green Goddess alocasia
    (Alocasia 'Green Goddess'), **118**
Growing conditions
    air circulation, 70
    bathrooms, 46
    bedrooms, 45
    halls and entryways, 42–43
    heat and humidity, 69–70
    indoors, 10, 42–49
    kitchens, 47
    living rooms and dining rooms, 43–44
Growing stand, how to build, **62–63**
Guzmania
    lingulata 'Orange Star', **134**
    lingulata 'Rana', **135**
    zahnii (poker plant), **135**

H

Haemanthus katherinae,
    aka Scadoxus multiflorus ssp. katherinae
        (fireball, Catherine wheel), **113**
Haitiora rosea, see Rhipsalidopsis rosea
Hanging plants
    general types, 21
    hardware for hanging, 51
    how to install supports for, **56–57**
    list of, 51
Hedera helix (English ivy), **114**
Heliconia psittacorum (parrot plant), **177**
Herbs, culinary, **49**
    growing indoors, 48
Hilo Beauty colocasia
    (Colocasia 'Hilo Beauty'), **120**
Hippeastrum (amaryllis), **113**
Homalomena rubescens 'Emerald Gem', **122**
Houseplants
    buying, 40–41
    choosing, 34–49
    examining before buying, 41

growing conditions, 10, 42–49
    high-humidity, 69
    leaf size and shape, 38
    leaf and flower color, 38–39
    raising and grooming, 58–77
    shape and growth habit, 36
    size, 35
Hoya carnosa
    (wax plant, porcelain flower), **141**
Humidity
    for seeds, 80
    heat and, 69–70
    maintaining for long period, 76–77
    plants that dislike dry conditions, 69
Hydrangea (Hydrangea macrophylla), **179**
Hydrangea family (Hydrangeaceae), **179**
Hypoestes phyllostachya,
    aka H. sanguinolenta
        (polka dot plant), **109**
Hypocyrta nummularia,
    see Nematanthus gregarius

I

Insecticidal soap, 101
Insecticide, use and storage, 102
Insects
    beneficials, 99
    control, 100–101
    pests, 98
Ivy
    for hanging, 21
    English (Hedera helix), **12**, **114**
    Swedish (Plectranthus australis), **182**

J

Jade tree (Crassula ovata), **140**
Jasmine, Madagascar
    (Stephanotis floribunda), **182**
Java tulip (Curcuma species), **157**
Justicia brandegeana (shrimp plant), **110**

K

Kaempferia rotunda (resurrection lily), **157**
Kaffir lily (Clivia miniata), **12**, **112**
Kalanchoe
    beharensis (felt bush, velvet leaf), **142**
    blossfeldiana (starfire kalanchoe), **142**
    thyrsiflora (dinner-plate kalanchoe), **142**

L

Ladybird beetles (ladybugs)
    beneficial insect, 99
Ledebouria socialis (silver squill), **163**
Licuala grandis (Chinese fan palm), **173**
Light
    artificial and sun-, 28–29
    daylengths, 58–59
    window, 59
Lighting, accent, 33
Lily family and relatives
    (Liliaceae), 14, **158–163**

Lipstick plant
    (Aeschynanthus spp.), **21**, **51**, **152**
    as hanging plant, 51
Lollipop plant (Pachystachys lutea), **110**

M

Madder family (Rubiaceae), **180**
Mallow family (Malvaceae), **180**
Mammillaria celsiana, aka Mammillaria
    muehlenpfordtii (globe cactus), **143**
Mandevilla × amabilis (dipladenia), **178**
Maranta family (Marantaceae), **181**
Mealybugs, identifying, **98**
    controlling, 100–101
Medicine plant (Aloe vera), **158**
Medinilla magnifica (pink grape plant), **181**
Melastoma family (Melastomaceae), **181**
Milkweed family (Asclepiadaceae), **182**
Mint family (Labiatae), **182**
Monstera deliciosa (Swiss cheese plant), **123**
Mites, see spider mites
Mosaic plant (Fittonia verschaffeltii), **109**
Moses-in-a-boat (Rhoeo spathacea), **174**
Moth orchid (Phalaenopsis hybrid), **170**, **171**
Mulberry family (Moraceae), 14, **164–165**

N

Nematanthus gregarius,
    aka Hypocyrta nummularia
        (goldfish plant), **153**
Neoregelia
    carolinae forma tricolor
        (striped neoregelia), **136**
    hybrid (blushing bromeliad), **137**
    'Royal Burgundy'
        (Royal Burgundy bromeliad), **136**
    spectabilis (fingernail plant), **137**
Nephrolepis
    exaltata 'Fluffy Ruffles'
        (Fluffy Ruffles Boston fern), **150**
    exaltata 'Timii', **150**
Nephthytis hybrid, **123**
Nolina recurvata,
    see Beaucarnea recurvata
Norfolk Island pine
    (Araucaria heterophylla), **176**

O

Orange Star bromeliad
    (Guzmania lingulata 'Orange Star'), **17**, **134**
Orchid family (Orchidaceae), 19, **166–171**
    decorating in masses, 27
    × Burrageara 'Stefan Isler'
        (Stefan Isler orchid), **166**
    Cattleya
        guatemalensis, aka C. deckeri
            (Guatemalan orchid), **166**
        hybrid (corsage flower), **166**
    × Colmanara 'Wildcat'
        (Wildcat orchid), **167**
    Cymbidium 'Jill Katalinca', **167**

× *Degarmoara* 'Stars 'n' Bars'
  (Stars 'n' Bars orchid), **167**
Dendrobium
  antennatum (antelope orchid), **168**
  bullenianum (topaz dendrobium), **168**
Epidendrum stamfordianum, **168**
Oncidium
  maculatum 'Paolo',
    (dancing lady orchid), **169**
  'Sharry Baby' (Sharry Baby orchid), **169**
Paphiopedilum
  insigne (lady slipper orchid), **169**
  'Red Sky' (Red Sky lady slipper
    orchid), **170**
  sukhakulii, **170**
Phalaenopsis hybrid (moth orchid,
  dogwood orchid), **170; 171**
Sophrolaeliocattleya Hazel Boyd 'Sunset'
  (orange cattleya), **171**
Zygopetalum crinitum (winter orchid), **171**
Other families (plant profiles), **176–184**

P

Pachyphytum plant
  (*Pachyphytum* species), **143**
Pachystachys lutea
  (lollipop plant, yellow shrimp plant), **110**
Painted nettle (*Coleus blumei*), **182**
Palm family (Palmae), **15, 172–173**
  bamboo (*Chamaedorea erumpens*), **172**
  butterfly
    (*Chrysalidocarpus lutescens*), **15, 173**
  Chinese fan (*Licuala grandis*), **15, 173**
  fishtail (*Caryota mitis*), **172**
  lady (*Rhapis excelsa*), **173**
  ponytail (*Beaucarnea recurvata*), **159**
Parodia penicillata (ball cactus), **144**
Parrot plant (*Heliconia psittacorum*), **177**
Peace lily (*Spathiphyllum* 'Domino'), **125**
Peat pots, **78–79**
Pedestals, for plant display, **55**
Pelargoniuim × *hortorum* (geranium), **179**
Pellaea rotundifolia (button fern), **150**
Pellionia repens
  aka *Elatostema repens*
    (watermelon begonia), **129**
Pentas lanceolata (Egyptian star cluster), **180**
Peperomia
  obtusifolia (trailing peperomia), **183**
  scandens (common peperomia), **183**
Pepper family (Piperaceae), **183**
Persian shield plant
  (*Strobilanthes dyerianus*), **111**
Persian violet (*Exacum affine*), **178**
Pests, insects, **75, 98–99**
Philodendron
  squamiferum, **124**
  'Xanadu', **124**
Pineapple plant, variegated
  (*Ananas cosmosus* 'Variegatus'), **133**
Pink grape plant (*Medinilla magnifica*), **181**

Plant profiles
  how to read, **107**
  major families, **108–175**
  other families, **176–184**
Plectranthus australis (Swedish ivy), **182**
Plume plant, yellow
  (*Aphelandra squarrosa*), **108**
Poelmanii flaming sword
  (*Vriesea* × *poelmanii*), **139**
Poinsettia (*Euphorbia pulcherrima*), **18, 147**
Poker plant (*Guzmania zahnii*), **135**
  yellow poker plant (*Vriesea* hybrid),
    17, 138
Polka dot plant
  (*Hypoestes phyllostachya*), **11, 109**
Polyscias
  fruticosa (ming aralia), **114**
  scutellaria 'Balfourii', aka *P. balfouriana*, **115**
Porcelain flower, *see* wax plant
Pothos (*Epipremnum*, aka *Philodendron* and
    Scindapsus)
  Marble Queen (*Epipremnum aureum*
    'Marble Queen'), **121**
  Satin (*Epipremnum* 'Satin'), **12, 122**
Pots
  cachepots, **54**
  for propagating, **78**
  glazed, **53**
  peat, **78–79**
  plastic, **53**
  terra cotta, **52–53**
Potting, **65**; *see also* Repotting
Powdery mildew, **103**
Prayer plant
  (*Calathea majestica* 'Roseolineata'), **181**
Praying mantid, beneficial insect, **99**
Primrose family (Primulaceae), **183**
Problems
  diseases, **102–103**
  insects, **99–101**
  poor care, possible causes, **97**
Propagating,
  by air layering, **90**
  bulbs, **91**
  covered unit, for, **79**
  cuttings, **86–89**
  by division, **84–85**
  growing medium for seeds, **79–80**
  humidity for seeds, **80**
  methods and hints, **94–95**
  using recycled containers for, **79**
  seed, **78–82**
  with seed pellets, **79**
  temperature for, **80–81**
  vegetative, **83**
Pteris cretica (Cretan brake fern), **151**
Purple heart plant (*Setcreasea pallida*), **15, 175**

R

Radermachera sinica (China doll plant), **177**
Remedies, insect control, **100–101**
Repotting, **66–67**
  care after, **67**

  instructions, **66**
  seedlings, **82**
  tools, **67**
Resting, to restore energy, **74**
Resurrection lily (*Kaempferia rotunda*), **157**
Rhipsalidopsis rosea, aka *Hatiora rosea*
  (Easter cactus), **144**
Rhipsalis species (pencil cactus), **144**
Rhoeo spathacea, aka *Tradescantia spathacea*
  (Moses-in-a-boat, Moses-in-the-cradle),
    174
Rosa chinensis 'Minima' (miniature rose), **184**
Rose family (Rosaceae), **184**
Rubber plant, Burgundy
  (*Ficus elastica* 'Burgundy'), **14, 165**
Rumohra adiantiformis (leather fern), **151**
Runners, planting, **83**

S

Sago palm (*Cycas revoluta*), **177**
Sanchezia nobilis, *see Sanchezia speciosa*
Sanchezia speciosa, **111**
Saintpaulia cultivars (African violet), **153**
Saxifraga sarmentosa, *see S. stolonifera*
Saxifraga stolonifera, aka *S. sarmentosa*
  (strawberry begonia), **185**
Saxifrage family (Saxifragaceae), **184**
Scadoxus multiflorus ssp. *katherinae*,
  see Haemanthus katherinae
Scale, identifying, **98**
Schefflera
  actinophylla 'Variegata'
    (variegated umbrella plant), **115**
  elegantissima, *see Dizygotheca elegantissima*
Schlumbergera
  × *buckleyi*, aka *Zygocactus*
    (Christmas cactus), **145**
  truncata (Thanksgiving cactus), **145**
Scilla socialis, *S. violacea*, *see Ledebouria socialis*
Scindapsus, *see Epipremnum*
Seasonal care
  bringing plants indoors, **75**
  fall, **75**
  summer, **74**
  taking plants outdoors, **75**
Sedum morganianum (donkey's tail), **146**
Seed pellets, **79**
Seedlings, transplanting and repotting, **82**
Seeds
  germinating, **80–81**
  propagating, **78–82**
Senecio macroglossus (wax vine), **184**
Setcreasea pallida, aka *Tradescantia pallida*
  (purple heart plant), **175**
Shapes, characteristic, **37**
Shield plant (*Alocasia* × *amazonica*), **116**
Shooting star (*Cyclamen persicum*), **183**
Shrimp plant (*Justicia brandegeana*), **110**
  yellow shrimp plant
    (*Pachystachys lutea*), **110**

Silver squill (*Ledebouria socialis*), **163**
Sinningia hybrid (gloxinia), **154**
Smithiantha speciosus (temple bells), **154**
Soap, to treat infested plants, 101
Soil, recipes, 64; types of, **64**, 80
Solenostemon scutellarioides, see Coleus blumei
Spathiphyllum
    'Domino', **125**
    floribundum (white-flag plant), **125**
Spider mites, identifying, **98**
Spider plant (*Chlorophytum comosum*), **160**
    for hanging, 51;
    planting runners, 83
Spiderwort family (Commelinaceae),
    15, **174–175**
Spotlights, to display and help plants grow, 33
Spotted ox tongue plant
    (*Gasteria bicolor* var. *liliputana*), **14, 162**
Stands
    for displaying, 55
    how to build a knockdown
      growing stand, 62–63
Stapelia gigantea (starfish flower), **146**
Starfish flower (*Stapelia gigantea*), **146**
Stephanotis floribunda
    (Madagascar jasmine), **182**
Strawberry begonia (*Saxifraga stolonifera*), **184**
Streptocarpella Cape primrose
    (*Streptocarpus* hybrid), **155**
Streptocarpus hybrid
    Streptocarpella Cape primrose, **155**
    Cape primrose, **155**
Striped neoregelia
    (*Neoregelia carolinae* forma *tricolor*), **136**
Strobilanthes dyerianus
    (Persian shield plant), **11, 111**
Succulents, *see* Cactus
Sunflower family (Compositae), **184**
Swedish ivy (*Plectranthus australis*), **182**
Swiss cheese plant (*Monstera deliciosa*), **123**
Syngonium podophyllum
    (Arrowhead plant), **126**
Syrphid fly, beneficial insect, **99**

T

Tachinid fly, beneficial insect, **99**
Tailflower (*Anthurium hookeri*), **118**
Temple bells (*Smithiantha speciosus*), **154**
Thanksgiving cactus
    (*Schlumbergera truncata*), **145**
Ti plant (*Cordyline terminalis*), **160**
Tillandsia
    cyanea (plume bromeliad), **137**
    ionantha (tufted bromeliad), **138**
Tobacco tea, used to kill scale, 101
Track lights,
    to display and help plants grow, 33
Tradescantia
    see Setcreasea pallida, Rhoeo spathacea,
      Zebrina pendula **174–175**

Trailing peperomia
    (*Peperomia obtusifolia*), **183**
Transplanting seedlings, 82
Trichocereus candicans, aka *Echinocereus
    candicans,* (torch cactus), **146**
Trimming and grooming, 72–73
Tulip
    Orange (*Costus curvibracteatus*), **156**
    Siam (*Curcuma alismatifolia*), **156**

U

Umbrella plant, variegated
    (*Schefflera actinophylla* 'Variegata'), **12, 115**
Urn plant (*Aechmea fasciata*), **132**
    silver (*Aechmea chantinii* hybrid), **17, 132**

V

Violet
    for hanging, 51
    African (*Saintpaulia* cultivars), **153**
    Flame (*Episcia cupreata*), **152**
    Persian (*Exacum affine*), **178**
Vriesea
    hybrid (yellow poker plant), **138**
    × *poelmanii* (poelmanii flaming sword),
      139
    splendens (flaming sword), **139**

W

Wandering Jew (*Zebrina pendula*), **175**
    Brazilian wandering Jew
      (*Callisia repens*), **15, 174**
Water damage, preventing, 24
Watering,
    from the bottom, 68
    overhead, 68
    self-watering methods, 76–77
    spraying, to dislodge pests, 100
Watermelon begonia (*Pellionia repens*), **129**
Wax plant (*Hoya carnosa*), **141**
Wax vine (*Senecio macroglossus*), **184**
Weeping fig (*Ficus benjamina*), **164**
White-flag plant
    (*Spathiphyllum floribundum*), **125**
Whitefly, **75**; identifying, **98**

X

Xanthosoma lindenii (Angel's wings), **126**

Y

Yellow plume plant, *see* Zebra plant
Yucca elephantipes (spineless yucca), **163**

Z

Zantedeschia
    elliottiana (golden calla lily), **127**
    rehmannii (pink calla lily), **127**
Zebra plant, aka yellow plume plant
    (*Aphelandra squarrosa*), **108**
Zebrina pendula, aka *Tradescantia zebrina*
    (wandering Jew), **175**
Zygocactus, see Schlumbergera × *buckleyi*

Photo Credits

Have a home gardening, decorating, or improvement project? Look for these and other fine **Creative Homeowner books** wherever books are sold.

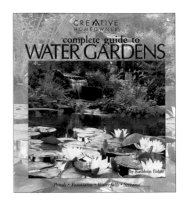
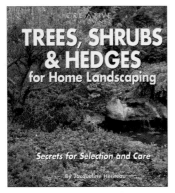

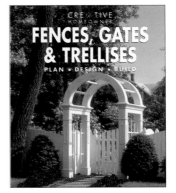
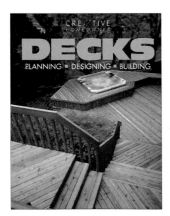
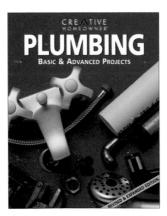

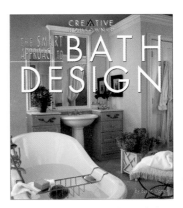